Wilson

by the same author

FICTION:

THE OLD RELIGON

THE VILLAGE

NON-FICTION:

THREE USES OF THE KNIFE

JAFSIE AND JOHN HENRY

TRUE AND FALSE

MAKE-BELIEVE TOWN

THE CABIN

ON DIRECTING FILM

WRITING IN RESTAURANTS

POETRY:

THE CHINAMAN

THE HERO PONY

PLAYS:

BOSTON MARRIAGE

THE CRYPTOGRAM

THE OLD NEIGHBORHOOD

OLEANNA

NO ONE WILL BE IMMUNE

GOLDBERG STREET

GLENGARRY GLEN ROSS

AMERICAN BUFFALO

A LIFE IN THE THEATRE

SPEED-THE-PLOW

THE WOODS, LAKEBOAT, EDMOND

SEXUAL PERVERSITY IN CHICAGO *and* THE DUCK VARIATIONS

SCREENPLAYS:

STATE AND MAIN

THE SPANISH PRISONER *and* THE WINSLOW BOY

HOMICIDE

HOUSE OF GAMES

WE'RE NO ANGELS

WILSON

A Consideration of the Sources

DAVID MAMET

Containing the original Notes, Errata, Commentary, and the Preface to the Second Edition

THE OVERLOOK PRESS
WOODSTOCK & NEW YORK

First published in the United States in 2001 by
The Overlook Press, Peter Mayer Publishers, Inc.
Woodstock & New York

WOODSTOCK:
One Overlook Drive
Woodstock, NY 12498
www.overlookpress.com
[for individual orders, bulk and special sales, contact our Woodstock office]

NEW YORK:
141 Wooster Street
New York, NY 10012

♾ The paper used in this book meets the requirements for paper permanence as described in the ANSI Z39.48-1992 standard.

Library of Congress Cataloging-in-Publication Data

Mamet, David.
Wilson : a consideration of the sources / David Mamet. —1st ed.
p. cm.
"Containing the original notes, errata, commentary, and the preface to the second edition."
1. Internet—Fiction. 2. Learning and scholarship—Fiction. I. Title
PS3563.A4345 W55 2001 813'.54—dc21 2001036016

Manufactured in the United States of America
FIRST EDITION
1 3 5 7 9 8 6 4 2
ISBN 1-58567-189-4

Contents

oh hey oh ho ye carrion crowe
ye kistrel ca' th' crowe awae
ye cuttie wren leuked doun a span
anent th' wanworth weurks o' man
ye linnet skiffed th' low-cut haye
aboun th' rick ye jay

Preface to the Second Edition
The Editors of *Bongazine*

It is not enough, I feel, to refer to these investigations as "Tales of the Old Wrangler."

Granted, the appellation could be stretched to fit; but one might, with as much justification, condense the whole of human history to "Anecdotes of the Famous and Misguided."

Yes, certainly, the following *do* and *must* treat (either directly, or by implication) of the Old Wrangler, but, more usefully, they deal with Krautz.

The growth of Krautz's canon, beginning with the Cola Riots, can be seen to parallel the settlement of Mars; he has, in fact, been identified (under the *nom de guerre* of Bennigsen)* with Mars, the God of War of the Ancient Geeks.

It is this *quality* to which we have directed our efforts.

The period of the Riots was known to its most immediate historians as the "Time of the Destruction of All Knowledge." But what, finally, was this destructive force?

Any schoolchild would answer, "The transfer of human literature into computer form, and its subsequent and accidental erasure"; and this was, of course, the response required by how many generations of scholastics.[1]

This would not, however, have been the response of a contemporary.

For a contemporary would have "known" that that "destruction" was caused not by the loss of "computer knowledge," but by the subsequent destruction of the Library and Stop 'n' Shop.[2]

1 – Bobs Merril, *Two Trains are Leaving Chicago* (Chicago, 2123).
2 – Treated here both *per se* and, in mythologic form, as "The Death of Chet and Donna."

---

* Or was *Krautz* the pseudonym?

It was the Great Decampment which began the "Change," as the last links were severed between our age and the "Written Word."[3]

This is the time which I would call that of the Great Romanticism – in which everything "left behind" was *per se* good.

But for this nostalgomania to function, it was necessary, of course, for things to *be* left behind.

And the Destruction of All Knowledge, whether occasioned by the Great Crash, or by the Fire, is, finally, a literary fiction.

For *all* knowledge, of course, *was not lost.*

What was lost?

That which is always lost, in the transition from one age to another, from one life to another, from one mood to the next, *et cetera*: something. Something. But not all. "All" was but a sentimental fiction, occasioned or necessitated, again, by the cognitive dissonance itself occasioned by the move to Mars. It has been written that the move from the Malls to Mars was, finally, "no great big deal"; but I cannot think that was the case.

It is my thesis that the literature "salvaged" equals, or *must* equal, the literature "created" – that it is not for nothing that these fragments survived, that their survival is *as* significant as would have been their creation, and that they must be taken as the *ding an sich* – as, if you will, the literature, mythology, or "Collective Memory" of that era.

For, yes, they treat of the Old Wrangler – as what does not? – but let us lay aside (let us say, for those readers of – and we do not disparage it – a religious turn) the (certainly true) notion of the Demiurge, and conjecture the existence of an independent consciousness or spirit, and we will call it the "Mind of Man."[4] Such, being by definition imperfect, must be other-than-unitary, must be mosaic; let us call its components "thoughts."

These "thoughts," these atomic, these irreducible "building

3 – Though an impartial survey of the scholastic blather published on "The Loss of the Written Word" might send one to the dictionary to double-check the definition of "oxymoron."

4 – Surely even the most vehemently fundamentalist must grant (if only hypothetically) the existence of such, else how explain gin?* (See S. Bronfman, *B'lieve I'll Have a Drink: History of Canada.*)

* But perhaps that is a question for another day.

blocks" of *consciousness*, must, again by definition, be, in themselves, incomplete.

The urge to order these "thoughts" is that which separates *Homo s.* from the lower orders. The urge to cease from doing so unites us with them.

So, then, yes, one might say, Bennigsen and Krautz *are* One; or, the Dog on the Capsule *was* the Toll Hound.

But *were* they One? What *was* the role of Jacob Cohen in the development of the Bootsie Clubs, and (though one has heard it innumerable times, I ask it again): What Became of Ginger?

It was the Wrangler himself who said that all was "Combination, Dissolution, or the Pause Between the Two";[5] and these peregrinations, misguided, as must finally be, like all human endeavor, in my consignment of them to the written page, and, thus, to the Collective Unconsciousness, for all that they are an attempt to unify-through-analysis (for what other tool does the historian have?), must themselves, at the end of the day, being "yet another term," finally but add to the burden of the reader–student, for which my apologies.

Was "All Knowledge" lost?

Had that been the case, how could one have made the assertion?

5 – *The Moving Picture Boys in Earthquake Land* (Boston, 1921).

Invocation

Invocation

O, ye exalted nine,[1] smile upon me!

1 – Or "mime."[A]

A – See also *Problems in Orthography: The Pocket Guide to the M–N Transposition in Ugartic, Ugantic, and Urdu* (The Handy Dandy Jack-a-Pandy "Little Giant of Philology" Books with the Yellow Cover).

For a fuller discussion of which see Rolly Nay, *Color as Trademark, or Eastman Kodak and the Three Bears*. This magnificent (and very funny) work explores the relationship between the collateral branch of the Warburg family and the "King of Rochester." I quote, with permission:

In he came, his arms full of Christmas presents.

Ross met him in the hall, bowing with his usual grace, and relieved him first of the encumbering packages, and then of his sable coat.

"How was your day, Mister E.?" Ross asked.

His only answer was a sad shake of the head.

"Troubles down th' fact'ry, sir?" Ross asked, and was surprised to see his employer, that rock, that stalwart, overcome by tears.

Ross led him to his "evening" chair, by the fire, in the salon. He retired only long enough to pass instructions to a parlour maid. "You have Cook bring his toddy," he said, and turned back, to see Charles Eastman, feet drawn up beneath him, curled into the big brown leather chair, his back heaving as the grief, as the frustration which he could not hide reduced him to the state of a child.

"What *is* it, Mister E.?" Ross said. "You *know* it doesn't do 'ny good to 'keep it in.' What is it, sir?"

"I can't . . . I can't . . . I can't . . ." the big man said, "I just can't find the perfect color to wrap my film in."

"What have you tried?" Ross quietly asked.

"I've tried them *all*," Eastman sobbed. "I've tried them all . . ."

"Have you tried *yellow*, sir . . . ?" Ross said.

The ensuing chapter, "The Best Christmas Present of Them All", is omitted here solely because of limitations of space. It would be an error to impute its omission to any other motive.

A Consideration of the Sources

A Consideration of the Sources
The Burden of the Argument

It must be noted that the phrase "it goes without saying" can be applied only to those things which are about to be conclusively demonstrated to require utterance.

Is the historian, then, a vulture, a scavenger or eater-of-broken-meats, to wait, induced, like the hyena, to a diet of carrion, subordinated to those rendered mighty over him by the mere accident of previous birth?

And yet, were we to abjure Sloppy Seconds in the practice of our craft – upon what would we practice it?

For must we not operate upon that, and *exclusively* upon that to which our attention has been drawn?

The classes of phenomena, then, forming our raw material, may be said to be two: those things of which we have been informed, and those things which no one has noticed.

The former being, by its very nature, productive of but few of the rewards historically associated with the practice of history, the historian is, it will be seen on scant reflection, forever preoccupied in a search, not for the true, but for the novel – his sole criterion, finally, "*That's* never been said before!", thus warping his craft and vitiating any benefits possibly derived therefrom in exchange for the specter of a momentary and possibly false sense of security derivative of his right of proprietorship in "the New", and the chimerical notion that such would produce "a lasting fame."

What folly are the Works of Man. For what could it avail one to have spent one's time and powers to this end: to achieve the prospective momentary approbation of the yet unborn.

And, should the endorsement of that far-off time prove more than passing, to what immediate strife and vexation would it not decay, enticing now this one, now that, again like hyenas, to claw, to tear, to bite their way into what now would have become, and been ratified as, the succulent body of a New Truth.

I cite the revelation in 2019 concerning the fingernails.

It had, of course, long been known that the fingernails continue to grow after death.

In 2019 an associate of Bennigsen (Greind) published a monograph – of which, of course, only a fragment remains.

Greind set out to establish under laboratory conditions that which had been held to exist, previously, only as – in the pejorative phrase of the time, "anecdotal information": that the fingernails do, *indeed, et cetera.*

His findings – which, I caution, have yet to be duplicated or recognized by any generally accepted scientific body – announced that not only do the fingernails continue to grow after death, but they grow at a rate 108 per cent of that at which they grow during life.

In searching for the exact moment of increased growth (brain death, heart death, etc.) – the signaling or triggering mechanism, as it were[1] – his team found this: that the nails ceased to grow at death, and began to grow again (at the increased rate) after a short period of inactivity.

Further attempts to fix the moment of increased activity caused the group to enlarge its investigations into the field of "near death," in which efforts they found, in the celebrated incident,[2] that the nails had ceased their growth some time *previous* to death; and, in fact, that cessation of their growth was an infallible prognosticator of an imminent demise.

The team's research having been both lost and discredited, government funding ceased, and we are left with just the tantalizing quirky pamphlet[3] and the survival, in our day, of the otherwise incomprehensible affection for calves'-foot jelly.

Let us proceed to the Poem.

1 – Bart Greind (ed.), *Laugh Till I Cry* (University of Indiana Press).
2 – *Captain Bob and the Campfire Girls in Earthquake Land et seq.*
3 – *Told You So* (Santeria World, autumn 2028).

The Poem Itself

The Poem Itself

Dawn, and the nascent, roseate glow.
Friend, if thou art Friend, perchancèd Foe,
Stand with me in the Light which sootheth all,
Suffusing the now ended slumbers on The Mall.

Only conceive, if it is granted thee,
Those noted years of bootless Misery,
The trials of the Heads of State,
The ceaseless Perturbation of the Great,

The ponderous burden of the few
To license, nay, inaugurate the new
Peregrinations of the Wandering Jew.

But for a moment meditate, I pray,
But for a moment stay.
Encapsulate the figures carved in stone,
Picture the absent flesh, the buried bone,
Hear with your inner hearing that fell tone
Of those controlled by Lust alone,
Of those whom neither shame nor pride debars
From luxury in the vermilion sway of Mars.
Apostrophize, if you will, on the thrall
Of History, and upon the futility of all.

Then may my eyes meet yours. And, for that while,
O, brother, may we not essay a smile?
Lost in the maelstrom of time,
Linked for a heartbeat sublime

Held for the sake of what O'erarching All –
Of what imponderables burnt –
Upon the deepest revelation of them all . . .

Authorship of the Poem

How oft have we said, of this or that, "it was right before my eyes"? And is not the greatest scholarship that which, with no reference to the arcane or abstruse, indicates to the common understanding that which, ever after, must be seen as self-evident?

The Poem on the Bookmark has, of course, long been held a piece of doggerel, important as "found in the Stop 'n' Shop" – a souvenir, if you will, of that day, an example of the *incunabula* of the pre-Riots mind.

And it was as such that I perused it[1] when a *pattern* began to shape itself before me.

Reader, what is Time? Or, to solicit a, perhaps, less lengthy answer, may not our (so human) predilection for "cause and effect" bar us from a, if not deeper, at least different, perception?

Could it not be that "reason," in the case, is (as has been suggested before)[2] "the enemy of truth," and that the most fell and unfortunate opponent of Free Thought is *neither* Government *nor* Religion, but, yes, but, the Calendar?

Could it not be, dear Reader, that we labor neath a monstrous, a delimiting temporal prejudice?

I will draw your attention to the Poem's final line, traditionally rendered:

Upon the deepest revelation of them all . . .

A prior time made much of the acrostic (the first letters of the last stanza, of course, read "TOLLHOU"). And the neo-Formalists[3] found comfort in conflating this, a (seeming) adumbrative reference to the

1 – Editions Suhrkampf, 15th fol., Neue Deutschland.
2 – The works of Victor Hugo.
3 – 2011–95.

Toll Hound, with that acrostic of the *first* stanza (DFSS, the first line of "code" written in Mrs. Wilson's urine).

They* devoted much time, and their followers have dedicated much shelf space, to the search for "the Last Two Letters" (i.e., those two final lines, that cadenza, which would supply the "ND", and round out the anagram to its complete "TOLL HOUND."

They would draw your attention to the seventeenth line:

. . . the buried bone

as further "proof" of the poem's essential *caninity*, and, thus, its authorship by Bootsie.[4]

While the Cohanim, of course, animadverted upon the Formalists' error, identifying the Wandering Jew as Jacob Cohen (himself, of course, in "the vermilion sway of Mars").

The Sensualists have put forward their thesis that the poem is either a construction of or a paean to their ilk, alleging "those controlled by Lust alone" must and can only be *Chet and Donna*, and that the Formalists were "a bunch of sesquipedalian motherfuckers."[5]

Their election of *Ginger*[6] upon such, to be generous, scant evidence, is a welcome tot of levity in this oft-times dry conversation.

And those of semantic–philologic bent have occupied themselves with the (necessary) rhyme(s) for "burnt," in what would be the poem's last two (missing) lines – the "ND" lines.

Reader, I meditated on the poem (which of us has not?) one winter afternoon.

I'd spent the morning in a trip to the coiffeur, and it had left my spirits unaccountably sad.

Returning to my garret, while I "pondered weak and weary,"[7] while the tea brewed, while the radiator hissed, while the shade snapped and fluttered in the more than occasional draft through the study windows – while life, in short, went on around me – I occupied

4 – See *The Hidden Meaning of the Bootsie Clubs* (Pleasantview Publications, New South Mars, 2111).

5 – Guest Book of the Ipatiev House.

6 – Jane Blaugh et al., *Of the World, Worldly* (Modicum House, New South Mars, 2211).

7 – Advertisement for Carter's Pills, 20??

* The neo-Formalists.

myself, I say, in thought, say, or in reverie or meditation, on "Those Times," the times of the Riots, and on the "Perturbation of the Great," the "burden of the few," *et cetera* – my thoughts ranging now to the micro, now to the larger levels of abstraction: who could have writ the poem? What did it "mean"? What were the missing lines?

And, as I sat, I must have shook my head, for I saw several small hairs fall to the page.[8]

One of these hairs, I saw, fell on the line: "Upon the deepest revelation of them all . . ." It fell between the "e" and the "m." And I saw that the last two words could be rendered "the Mall."

Can you conceive my beating heart, my flushed countenance, as I stared at that page?

How can the o'erfamiliar be transmuted – flax into gold – into the intuitive, revelatory, in an instant!

For, *were* it possible the poem referred to the Mall, the missing lines, then, must refer to its apotheosis.

For, you see, it is this "missing term", in retrospect, which must inform the poem. *Not* the identification, or the (real or imagined) homage to Chet, to Donna, to Ginger, to Bootsie, nor to the Wrangler Himself, no, but to Jane of Trent.

And I saw, if the "final" line were warped by a compositor's or proofreader's error, was it not possible – was it not *likely*, in fact – that an adjacent line was similarly warped?

Let us, then, admit that ". . . what imponderables burnt," with all and sundry overtures of peace and gratitude to its interpreters, can make sense "only at a stretch."

Could it not be that a lax, a sleepy, or unqualified compositor misset the word? Might the line not have been, might it not be more reasonable to understand or to accept it as, "Of what imponderables *blent*"? Bear with me, Reader, and conceive the sequence –

Held for the sake of what O'erarching All –
Of what imponderables blent –
Upon the deepest revelation of the Mall

8 – Although, as he'd written elsewhere (*Me 'n' Bootsie*, chapter 12), he had habitually asked them to "shampoo his hair" after a haircut.

– the last rhyme suggesting itself, ineluctably, dear Reader – and then, if the last rhyme, if the conclusion of the coda, if the tendency of the whole poem, then, is, as it must be, "Jane of Trent", must it not be that the last, "the deepest revelation of the Mall," is that of the poem's authorship, and that the author was Krautz?

Note

It is not for us to draw attention to the lacunae – for, if we were to begin, where end? I will only mention two of my favorite:

1 The "figures carved in stone," which popular and sustained scholarship, of course, identifies as Chet and Donna.
2 The failure of the author to pay the slightest attention to "encapsulate."

For, if we are not talking about – if the *author* cannot give *fair weight* to – the overarching presence of Chet and Donna; if he can ignore the – one could not call it "coy" – reference to the Capsule, then what the hell are we talking about here?[9]

9 – I will not tax the reader's time nor sense of outrage by referring to the omission (even if a "mere sop to Formalism") of a reference to "bootless Misery" as a homage to Bootsie.

The Riots

The Riots

> For in the cauldron of the times
> the alloy of the soul was forged
> [cooked]. TRADITIONAL

The populace had of course long suspected that all ethnic food was cooked in the one vast kitchen, and then trucked out and doused in that sauce which would identify it as Chinese, or Indonesian, Thai or what-have-you.

And much had been written – in that special vein beloved of that era, of conspiracy theory – of the indistinguishability, on close inspection, of the Democrat and the Republican view.

It was the staple of the age, in fact, that all things were alike, that all polarities were unities, that one would be well served to consider every solution as a problem, and every problem as a solution – that things, in short, were unfolding not only as they must, but happily; and that the detached viewer could observe their unfolding with jollity.

But the wry stoicism of the age was shattered, as we know, by the revelations that October.

Nothing of the discoveries of the amino-historiographers, neither the secret of Kennedy's suicide, nor the revelation of Wilson's sex, had the impact of the discovery that Coke® and Pepsi® were one.

It is a mistake, I feel, to refer to the "Riots."

I think closer examination might reveal three distinct stages, and that each might deserve our study as a discrete whole, and I am indebted, as are we all, to Franz Krautz, and his seminal "Woodrow Wilson: Vice Versa," for the paradigm, "Denial–Rage–Reaction."

I feel, however, the Krautzian Triad militates in favor of a unity which – as is the center of my thesis – may be lacking in that decade known to us as that of the "Cola Riots."

I first will take issue with the term *per se.*

It is, I feel, a flag of convenience, uniting, finally, arbitrarily, events arguably unconnected (e.g. "Bolivia," "deutero-Zoroatrianism," "Muuguu.")

And though the Decade of the Riots (in point of fact, of course, fourteen years) will accept the template "D–R–R", so will the rejected suitor, or the mis-seated diner forced to smoke.

Is it not, finally, the nature of perception to order any untoward event or series of events into the form D–R–R–A;[1] which tendency, if indulged, reduces and would reduce the task of both historian and, arguably, amino-historiographer to that of a mechanic.

For I, like Krautz, like Aristotle,[2] for that matter, advise that, finally, *any* event may be reduced to thirds and understood according to the formula, *Crack, Snapple, Pop*.[3]

I do not claim immunity from the foibles of the enthusiastic, nor from the endemic tunnel vision of the professional; and am well aware of the dictum of George Bernard Shaw that "all professions are conspiracies against the laity."[4]

I think the Decade of the Riots falls into stages not *only* distinct but (*pace* Professor Krautz) unconnected, or connected only by a common tinge of tragedy. By way of simile I would ask the reader to consider mourners from three different funerals misinformed, and arriving at a funeral home which houses the object of none of their obsequies.

These people would conjoin and exchange the amenities pertinent to the scene, and would, in time, come to share reminiscences and condolences and, so, to discover, finally, that they held nothing in common save the fact of their grief and the accident of their individual (*not* "communal") misapprehension.

Nor can we, at this remove, conceive the atmosphere of disbelief, chaos, and distrust of authority engendered by the Crash, preceding the Riots by a scant fifty years.

For, dating the birth of Edison in 1941,[5] and the Crash of the

1 – Where A = Acceptance. See Wayne Newton IX, *So What?* (University of Iowa Press, 2015).
2 – *The Poetics, or Dink Stover at Yale*, AD ?
3 – I am indebted to Morris Watkins Bane for the identification of *Snapple* and *Crack* as two late twentieth-century analgesics. Both common sense and recent philologic–semantic matrii reject the identification of *Pop* as a cognomen of Wernher von Braun. As do I.
4 – *The Young Lions*.
5 – J. Blota, *First See If It's Plugged In* (Mud Press, 2091).

Internet in 2021, we have a period of eighty or, in the words of the phone book,[6] "four score, thank you for calling" years of the reign of that commodity understood as "information," we have a scant ninteen years, the "time of the Troubles," before the Revelation, and the Riots. It is my contention to reverse the commonly understood relation of planet-to-satellite, and suggest that the rage expressed at the Revelation was not displacement from the Crash, but, rather, that the Crash was a warning shock, a mechanic adumbration of the spiritual and psychologic torment of the Revelation.

For it has been said that the beginning of wisdom is the ability to consider one's position as a thing separate from one's best interest.[7]

And the evaporation of that which the world came to call its "Information" was, in my view, a "loss-on-paper," while the Revelation and the suicide of Bart Greind touched a core of disaffection, "as old as the hills."

History offers many instances of the "incendiary incident." It is, in fact, axiomatic that a period of unrest be sparked into conflagration by the intolerable: the French Revolution brought to being by the peasants' rage at the destruction of the Bastille; World War II by France's furor at the intrusion of Lindbergh, etc.

The precepts of Psychic Economy instruct that the affect must be in adjustment to the stimulus.[8]

The ravages of the Decade of Riots cannot, in the light of reason, be linked to the demise of the "Information Age," which must, on reflection, be seen as nothing more or different than a (granted, large-scale) loss of memory. (One might as well say that a man came home and murdered his dog because he forgot where he moored his car.)

No, the Riots sprang into being "like Zeus from Leon's Head."

Their cause was cause enough, and even now one wonders if sufficient time has passed for rational assessment.

Be that as it may.

6 – For further work on the phone book, I direct the reader to Anon., *Funny Names, No Plot.*

7 – O. J. Stimson, *Think About It* (2002).

8 – Hillary Rodham Clinton Rodham, *Highsticking.*

The – as the reader has determined – anti-Krautzian bent of this article is neither historical nor amino-historiographic[9] but a cry for reason. I will suggest and explore the alternatives to the triadic view in chapter 2.

9 – Though I do suggest the application of the *Merck Manual*, 2091–92, and of the 92093 *Index*, and the obvious use of their formula for "carbon-based literal distillates." See Merck, op. cit., and *The Index* (Merck, DC Comics); and, by the way, the stunningly concise *At a Store Near You* by Antoinette and François Pope (University of Melanesia Publications, 2045), and, of course, the film *Bunny* based thereon. The transformation of the character Kal-El into the friendly Doctor Brown has become a part of the culture and needs no notice herein. I need refer only to the Doctor's likeness in bronze on the Mall facing the Mud Pond. And would like to take this opportunity to relate an aperçu connecting *not* the film but an incident *absent* in the film but *present* in the pamphlet that survived, like the poisons in medicine, in spite of efforts to eradicate it. It was during the third 'mester at the Mud Pond when I found myself, engaged in contemplation of an abstruse zine – the first, or "pirate", edition of *Jane of Trent*, bearing, for those of that bent, the renowned spot/pots transposition on page 12 – one evening, in short, before the fall Ordeal, when I found myself before the Doctor, and climbed on the plinth to rub his ears. I looked down, and saw, at some remove, a loved professor, sitting in his barge, and, as I thought, weeping copiously.

I moved to descend, and slipped and fell, sustaining a concussion which confined me to a hospital for several months, where I met the woman who was to be my wife.

Three into Twelve
Homage to the Triadic[1]

While it has been suggested that early skirmishes in the Whole-at-Cost split the Reform movement upon the issue of one- – or two- – day celebration of Rosh Hashanah, more contemporary and, I must say, to me, more convincing scholarship suggests that the issue of contention was the inclusion of beach-blanket bingo as an Olympic event.[2]

An idea so believed of its times as to be wellnigh insuperable, and

1 – Variant: Tribadic (disputed), *Smith College Anthology of Humor* (2211); see also *Funny Bathroom Signs of Wisconsin*, op. cit., and cf. "Ramifications of The Joke Code," p. 29.

2 – Robert Hastings-Burke, *I Left My Love in Avalon* (Pacific Rim Publications) and *You Like It, It Likes You: The Story of Martin Buber*, plus "When I hear the word 'Culture' I reach for my Browning Automatic," George Goebbels, *Lonesome George* (Bath Press, 1959); *Do You Know Where I Can Get Scrod?: The Depletion of the Grand Banks*; cf. *Captains Courageous*, with Spencer Tracy as the Beaver; "We're Here!" by Mr. Jacques of the Ritz, formerly of Brookline Cut 'n' Curl; and Anon., *Toot, Toot, Peanut Butter, or The Imaginary Rabbit* (p.d.) . . . mitigating toward the unitary, in defiance of the quasi-legal sway (certainly the popular primacy) of the 12-step program, Dodecanensis.[A, B]

A – See Paul H. Patt, *Dodecanensis or The Dozens in Action* (McGill University Press, 1948) (in the French translation, *Les Douzaines: Ta Soeur a ses Propres Raisons*), from which I quote (with permission):

. . . the small white house, the scent of mock-orange, hanging like a velvet drape in the summer evening heat, the ice-cream vendor's bell,[A1] "*Ding* dong, *ding* dong . . .", as Billy and Ginger thrust their chairs back from the dining table, and their "M'I'b's'cused?" came, almost as one syllable, and in unison from their mouths, as they ran from the house, out towards the ice-cream man.

Oh, if you could have been there, to see and to hear that screen door slam in that most American of all summer sounds, and to see sweet Tritzi, the wire-haired dachshund, caught out again, and staring through the screen.

What must the world have looked like to her, Ginger wondered, those long decades later, as she stared, at the world, through a different *kind* of screen . . . "*Two* screens," she thought: the mesh security fence and her psychosis.

A1 – See also "The Ice-cream Vendor's Bell", *The Poems of Hart Crane*.

"What a dog, however," she thought. "That's some kind of dog. In *spite* of that he was a Kraut."

White white white white, the sky went buttermilk.

"No, it's just white," she thought. And, ". . . Billy: Lookit!"

But he was gone. Into the street, hightailing toward the ice-cream truck, and did not hear the car horn, nor the squeal of brakes, nor the sick final impact, nor the silence afterwards, nor his mother's moans, nor see his father's resolution, nor the 1959 World Series, nor . . .

"Oh, stuff a *sock* in it!" the orderly screamed at Ginger, who, as always, didn't realize she had been thinking out loud.

Heaved out of her pleasant reverie, Ginger hawked up and spat, as was her wont, to the four cardinal points, and fell to the floor to curl in her usual "ball," knees to forehead, feet to buttocks, head to the south-south-west to avail herself of the afternoon sun's yellow rhomboids on the linoleum floor.

"Wherever would old Tritzi be now?" she wondered. "Dead. Of course. Long dead. Her flesh gone, her very bones, perhaps, gone, eaten by a cat, maybe; or, perhaps (*yuck*) by another dog . . .

"And where the hell is Billy, and, more to the point, the Hudson Terraplane with which Mrs. Beal ran him down . . .?"

("*That* put a hole in her shopping day," she thought, and chuckled.)

Now Marie, the nurse's aide, high-stepped over her, and glanced down at the spreading pool of urine. She shook her head.

"I hope to *hell* that I haven't got some on my *shoes*," she thought. "I hope to *hell* that I have not."

"Each of us, in his way, is a valuable citizen," said Ginger. "Even the dog. Although it only was his job to sit there and look wistful."

"Clean yourself up," Marie said.

"And *fuck* the Nazis," Ginger screamed. "Are we to demand *for ever* that their *dogs* pay for it . . .?"

Marie shook her head.

". . . they're hardly *human*. And look how they have to pick up the tab for their bad associations. Well," she screamed, "I guess we *all* do."

Marie walked to the broom closet. She opened the door, sighed, and pulled out her mop and pail.

B – The Traditional *Table of Organization of the Canon*[B1] ("Riot," to the Third Martian See) ran, of course:

Chet and Donna
Ginger
Jacob Cohen
The Old Wrangler
The Fantasist
The Redactor
Bootsie
The Toll Hound
Bingo
Bennigsen and Krautz

The Caninists traditionally conflated the Toll Hound and Bingo, as one of the "Six Working Pairs." Their error persisted, and they persisted in their error until and *in despite of Bongazine*'s publication of *The Settlement of Michigan* (p. 67).

The *correct* identification of Bingo as other-than-canine led to the recognition of the (to our eyes, obvious) *Bootsie–Bingo* alignment.

That such, however, left the Toll Hound "unpaired" went unremarked until the "Spring Annual" of *Bongazine*, 2101.[B2]

B1 – Oft considered the "key to section one" (*Ft. Worth Star–Dispatch*).
B2 – *"Jay Burrows into mass of Confectioner's Sugar: 'I was tired of being Blue'"*, etc.

found again and again in the paradigm of the helper–antagonist, as dwarves, disciples, graves-to-Cairo; and where we find the Krautzian Triad, on publication, scorned or the presentation (truth be told, of course, *championship*) of a psycho-numerology based upon the number three.

Much has, of course, been written of the attempts of apologists to expand and/or subdivide the triads. The classic of the genre being, of course, *Three into Twelve* by *George* Krautz[3] – of which admissible critical restraint and respect for the father militate against application of the verdict "craven."

3 – For an impartial appreciation of Krautz *fils*, I recommend *Ashes* by Mara Lentz, and its screen treatment, *Testament of Dust.*

Harsh as the life of a poet very well may be, we cannot help but recur to the words of Chief Justice Hugo Black in the decision *Marbury v. Madison Guarantee*, in which a medical man, summoned to minister to an expiring bank director, fell into a cistern. The Justice, writing for the majority opinion, commented: "He should have catered to the sick and left the well alone."

And it may not be amiss, having granted to the young Krautz the application for which he strove, that of a poet, to quote from a work, chosen, the reader may be free to believe, at random, *Pottery*:

Not unlike products from Japan
Innocent of all identifying marks
No pride of place
Informs the crockery of our soul.
No. Rather, like . . . [*et cetera*]

It took the genius of "Little Timmy Jones"[B3] to find inspiration in that disjunction. She reasoned that the "valence" (her word) of the Toll Hound suggested a "partner" of similar weight; such a "partner," she continued, was not to be found in the List of Twelve. *But such must exist.* It was her reasoning which led to the first recorded suggestion of the identity of Bennigsen and Krautz – such reducing the Pantheon to Eleven, and "Allowing the Mind to Rove,"[B4] till Modern Scholarship[B5] came to teeter, as it now does, upon that precipice beyond which we find, not "the void," but a (pardon the irony) belated recognition of the deity of Jane of Trent.

B3 – Mrs Ruth Moncrieff, "The Cedars," Newton Lower Falls, Mass.
B4 – *History of Whippies.*
B5 – See "Bunny" Gaye,[B5A] *Those "Little Men in Gold"* (The Learn-to-Read Foundation).

B5A – It was a "Bunny" Gaye who, while an undergraduate at Smith College, discovered the compositor's "miscorrection" of "homard" to "homage" in Marcel Duchamp's 1921 *Manifesto: Homage* au Dadaïsme.* (Small world.) (Pity about her marriage.)

---

* [Homard.]

Stick to your last, the Ancients cautioned. Can we doubt their wisdom? No. The history of Krautz *fils* has little interest outside the bathetic. For did he not, in his wretched endeavors now to escape, now to explain, his feeling for his father, merely reiterate those – if only those – aspects of the bond he deemed unfortunate?[4]

4 – From: Hugo Black, Chief Justice WBA, *Lettres de mon Moulin*:

A man is on a choochoo train traversing Russia. In the carriage with him is an old Jewish fellow, rocking interminably back and forth, and muttering, "Oi, am I thirsty," hours on end.

The train stops at a remote station, and our traveler, driven mad by the Jew, leaps from the train, runs into the station, and buys him a tasty drink.

Back in the train the Jew downs the drink (lemonade), the traveler settles back into his seat, sanguine the Jew will now subside to silence.

The train accelerates, and the Jew, however, begins once again to rock, intoning, this time, "Oi, was I thirsty, oi was I thirsty . . ."

Cf. Lynn Bogue Hung, *Billing and Cooing: The Economics of Prostitution in Twentieth-century Indiana* and *Porno-Economics: The Hurly Burly of the Chaise-longue* (Sportsman's Press), and Marcia Kelley, Brig. Gen. USAR Ret., *It's Not the Men, It's the Stairs.*

A Close Contemporary Allusion to "The Riots"[1]

Once he had sought, as had many before, in the "Unsorted Notes," and to the selfsame net effect. And once he had devoted himself to – it must be said to have surpassed an "interest," and, perhaps, even, an "obsession" – an identification with the Fantasist.

That, too, had passed. But each had formed the "thews and sinews" of his maturing intellectual constitution, and, in all his later works, their influence could be seen.

Consider the phrase "struck from the flint of his imagination."[2] The very use of the stock phrase, considered as such *even during the Time of the Riots,** is and must be considered as a jesting reference to the Fantasist. Its recrudescence[3] suggests, again, an (almost) pathologic involvement with the same.

It has been suggested that *Home Again to Pinky* can be read as a reverie upon "what might have been" had the Fantasist himself had access to the "Unsorted Notes." While this is, to this writer's mind, "a little hard to swallow," it is the specific *application* of the Theory of Obsession, and not, at all, its overall supportability *qua* diagnosis which is here pooh-poohed.

For, finally, he *was* obsessed. The very names of his pets[4] testify to the fact, as do the names of his retreats.[5]

1 – See also *Tales of the Fantasist*; *The Fantasist in Story and Song*; *[Children's] Life of the Fantasist*, also known as *Life of the Fantasist for Children*; and *Twenty-nine Palms after Dark*.

2 – *Idle Hours by Stream and Campside, Apologia* (The Whippies Corporation).

3 – "Struck like chain lightning from the rock of his consciousness," *Idle Hours Neath the Stars*; "smashed like the very dickens from the adamant of his awareness," *Idle Hours at Bath and Torquay*, etc. etc.

4 – Trish, Monkey, Two-for-the-Show (Champion Laeticia's Dragon-Dumfrey Loxen Box).

5 – Back 'n' Hidin', Kungsholm, Sproon.

---

* Emphasis in the original.

But so what?

"Each to his own," as the Wrangler had it, and "Whatever gets you [through][?][to][?] the Night."

To return –

Once he had sought in the "Unsorted Notes." Once he had "toyed" with the Fantasist. His works proclaim it, and that is the formulation I shall adopt in the second draft. Grace, pls take note. Thank you, P.

. . . his works proclaim it. But see if you can include the footnotes, P.

Strike out the section on the parking meter problem and put it later in the book. Thanx. P.

Did I remember to ask you to send flowers to Mrs. Nulty? And put in a reference, if you would, to "Friday night": thank you. P.

Do you think I could get these pages by *Monday*? If it will help, forget about that "other thing" – thanks a lot. P.

Ramifications of the Joke Code

One need not, unfortunately, refer to a time even as little remote as that of the Riots to discover inordinate savagery and inhumanity unbounded.

It is, if not a fashion, at least an accepted convention to compute or graph this or that enormity employing the formula, "Not since the time of the Riots."[1]

The above quotation, long a hobby-horse of the scholars and aficionados of the late Victorian period, cannot, unfortunately, be to a certainty translated to the modern mind. This is, of course, the yoke, burden, and secret shame of History – the degree to which she, even in her pose of jade, harlot, rough-trade, whore, slattern, etc., in which she allows the soupcan of certainty to be inferred, whilst, all the while, guarding her right of retreat to the safer ground of impartial

1 – "We did not have these pea green soups until people began to describe them." (O. Wilde)[A]

A – I fear I must take up the issue of the pea soup "joke" referred to in note 1. This "joke" has been fairly definitively identified thus:

SPEAKER: I will say various things to you, and you must respond, whatever I say: "French Canadian Pea Green Soup."

LISTENER: All right.

SPEAKER: What did the French Canadian have for breakfast?

LISTENER: French Canadian Pea Green Soup.

SPEAKER: What did the French Canadian have for lunch?

LISTENER: French Canadian Pea Green Soup.

SPEAKER: What did the French Canadian have for dinner?

LISTENER: French Canadian Pea Green Soup.

SPEAKER: What did the French Canadian do then?

LISTENER: French Canadian Pea[A1] Green Soup.

A1 – ("pee") The original (by Greind) was in *101 Joke Pranks, and Rainy Day Activities* (The Hardy Little Books with the Yellow Cover). That its discoverer was Greind can evoke neither doubt nor interest.

transcriber; the degree, I say (and that degree near totality), that degree, her profession of the same not to the contrary, to which she knows less than one goddamn thing. None the less, we here offer a *hint*, and abjure, in the offering, any and all claim to its production, assistance in the same, copyright either moral or legal, to any, in short, real or imagined benefit either existing or to exist accruing to the discovery here below.

Now, how could one do so, avoiding at all removes the possible assessment of "coyness," which (having lived long enough to've lost any residual hint whatever (had it existed) of a belief in the fairy tale of "human goodness"), I must assume, will be hurled at me by an intellectual and critical establishment the application of either adjective to which is a tragic joke?

BY NAMING THE PERSON WHO MADE THE DISCOVERY, AND TO WHOM ALL CREDIT MUST ACCRUE (see chapter 12).

The savagery to which I refer is, of course, that directed by the public (both *per se*, and, "in committee" – if you will – which is to say, as "the consensus of the learned," which is to say those craven, old, emasculated wretches of all sexes sitting on their duffs in Towers of Ivory both figurative, and, for all I care, actually fashioned from the teeth of elephants, and raining down reactive, misinformed and cowardly opinions on a world which, as it was created by God, might be said to've deserved better – that pathologic, cruel, that inexplicable save by reference to the Zoroastrian, mischief: THE DISMISSAL OF THE JOKE CODE AND THE MARGINALIZATION OF ITS PARTISANS ADHERENTS AND INVESTIGATORS.

Line them up against the wall, I say, and shoot them. For they have done bad, and they know it.

The Writer's Mind

The Writer's Mind

For, to know the cry is to know the dog. BOOTSIE

"U Thant," he had written, "take a goldfish for walks."[1]

Which notion we see again explored in the margin of the facing page as "You can't take a goldfish for walks, but you *can* take a goldfish for *one* walk. See page 12," on which page, "U Thant take a goldfish for wogs. Does it begin to break down there?" he muses. And, yet, again, "U Thant take a goldfish to wogs."

By which it must appear that, having subdued the flanks, there rests the problem of, as Clausewitz had it, the *Schwerpunkt*, upon which subject we must quote Alexander the Great.

He held that an attack upon the fortified center must and will demoralize the opposition, and grant the aggressor spiritual superiority (redeemable as victory-in-arms).

We must take him at his word, begging the question of the existence (Y/N?) of that antagonist, or deutero-self, that *Ur*-self, that psycho or psychotomimetic *Doppelgänger*, that respondent or "dear Reader," that "imaginary Friend," which is the, the the the, the the the the bollard to which the deranged or literary mind moors that craft (i.e. its imagination), in which it reposes its hope of seaworthiness.

How alike, might he* have said, are the two endeavors† – all compact of shit and stink, of rapine, pillage, of the setting-as-naught of compunction. What joy!

The offending term, then, "goldfish," presents itself for our contemplation.

How will he deal with it?

1 – *Miracle on 47th Street*, op. cit. Cf. *Miracle on 48th Street, Miracle on 49th Street*, and the, granted, less-though-not-anti-thaumaturgical, *Spurges Guides to New York* (The Little Yellow Book That Screams Out, "*Rob* Me!".) We are grateful to Miriam and Paul Spurges and the George and Anna Spurges Foundation for their benign [?complicity (illegible, Ed.)] in the production of this [?volume; ?vellum].

* Alexander. † Writing and war.

We see that it may be approximated in either its rhythm or its sound. An attempt to capitalize *solely* upon an introversion or "harmonic" in its meaning *absent* that obeisance to rhythm or sound (or rhythm-and-sound, in the perfect case) must traduce, we hold, any possible worth in the line-as-jest.

And here rests the problem. And here rests the problem. In the middle term. Where we see* "Goldstone. No. Goldberg. No. *Worldbank*" – the last word underlined three-several times, and followed with what he, in his enthused state, surely must have intended as an exclamation point.

For it was here he broke through, sacrificing the surety of the concept "Gold," for the greater good: the worth of the line.

He sacrificed what is (now) seen to've been the false term and stood, clean and whole, grasping in his hand, as if fresh returned from a journey to the Underworld – or to the bottom of the pond, or of the bathtub or what-have-you, some such metaphor for consciousness of some such "thing" – grasping, triumphantly, I say, if not the Completed Thing, that thing to the artist far superior, the sense of the way *to* that thing.

Not without, not without, I say, that sadness – not only remorse for the necessary excision of what *might* have been said, had its creator been more adept, gifted, inspired, rested, but, still, in sorrow for the state of a mind bent to such sick frivolity; a mind so bereft of order that it gropes and grasps and delights in the similarity in the accidental and useless, cobbling together such where such does not exist.

And sadness, too, for and at the simple act of completion, that post-coitum tristere known to all who've ever had their ashes hauled. But to return to the problem, which, as he saw it, rested, then,† in the unfortunate (to him, one may well suppose), insupportable lack of agreement between the proper noun (U Thant) and the verb, which, if the line is to have any worth and not merely rest as the recipient of that license a depraved world increasingly grants to the approximate to pass and pose as Art, must (one would have thought) must stand in the third person singular past tense.

That he *made* the world fresh for wogs lacks and must have lacked, of course, to his mind, both the "snap of recognition," which is the *sine*

* On the Notepad. † And now.

qua non of humor (which must, at the end of the day, be considered as nothing less than delight in derangement) and the labial and aural delights of the fricative.

Here, then, we may see him, as it were, "break through," and hit upon the device which "renders the whole thing whole," the solution to the content lying, as often it must, in the mastery of the problems of form.

His application of the colon, "U Thant*: make the world fresh for wogs" (as seen in pencil, in the margin) and the final "U Thant: make a bold wish for wogs" only just less memorable than the *postscriptum*, "Garbage day today. Going home."

* *U Thant*: Secretary General, Benighted Natives, 1968-?? See also: Camacho's, "*That Boogie in the Winter-O*." MAN'S BEST FRIEND, Macho Camacho, ed.

Dear Diary

Mentioned in *Whippies, or Life at a Long Remove* as being found in the Capsule;[1] cf. 'In the Capsule', p. 205.

Dear Diary,

I am surprised that I am surprised any more.

One would've thought that since that time we moved and the milkman moved with us that nothing in Mother's life or demeanor would have awakened anything save resignation.

But by such and by such only is philosophy attained.

Of what use is it, then?

We say it is good in itself. But is it not merely – if and as we examine its inception I fear we must say it is – an analgesic?

How much more preferable to've gone without the milk. (Though even at this (oh, so long) remove, I could regret the Double Gloucester . . .)

How we would prefer, each to have forgone the tragedy, the treason, the tests, the "life." In short (as Bishop Berkeley had it), to've lived unaware. In bliss. In a garden (though what better paradigm for death and decay, for transiency, and for corruption; for betrayal, treason, perfidy . . .?)

(I speak not here of her (increasingly frequent) retreats into the box hedge, the gazebo, with this or that retainer, schoolchild, tradesperson, horse-coper, gypsy, and so on, but of the more quotidian – the round of birth, anxiety, degeneration.)

These degenerations then, we might say, more than the "life" of the garden – they *are* the garden. *Toute entière*. The worms, the various blights, the aphids, moths, moles, rusts, frosts, drafts, supply, do they not, all one might need to know of application of that natural force which might as well be enmity, which, at the last, must be counted

1 – See Larry Budd, *Bookmarks and Ephemera of the Voyage Out*. See also: *A Guide to the Parking Meter Problem*, and *My Fantasist and Yours* (Faith Publications).

stiff-necked opposition and intent to persuade without guidance, without correction, unabashed – to grow in its own way and only in that way.

How like her wantonness – the record of which I would have thought incapable of further elaboration, but in which estimate I would have erred by what I must now admit to have been several orders of magnitude.

Et cetera.

January 25th, 19—

"I shall not wear the blue.

"I shall not wear the beige I shall not wear the kerseymere – I shall not wear the taupe nor the mauve. I shall not wear the lawn. I shall not wear the lavender – " and so the list continues, one would say interminably were it not that a glance down its rhythmed column reveals, as it must, an end.

An end, and that end shocking beyond any power one might have vouchsafed her (at this advanced date) to've shocked.

And neither do I approve of the craze for perennials, nor account it filial piety to continue in their cultivation.

A close observation, an extended contemplation of a flower bed yields nothing superior to a cursory one.

Granted, a stay in its environs can, by turns, soothe or refresh – but so can drink, in submission to which one does not risk self-application of the sobriquet "effete."

To return: how *can* one ingest or adapt to the unacceptable?

Through, only through a form of negotiation – no, it is not wisdom. It is not philosophy – there is no such thing. There is that fatigue born of repetition, hope deferred and the subsequent extinction of desire (yes, even the desire for revenge), and there is "time." And the negotiation takes place between "now," and "then" – "then" being both the past and future, the affront, and the eventual cessation of its sway – both juxtaposed against the present sordid and interminable moment of what might be felt as a self-sustained injury; for, as philosophy informs us: who continues to injure us? None but ourselves.

No, no. I will not follow her in her (twice nightly?) – yes, I find myself defending her: "... but only during dinner parties ..." – recursions to the topiary.

I will not "sniff," as it were – "sniff" nor otherwise examine the (to what end . . .?) flowered borders crushed beneath her (but *not solely* her) bulk.

Nor continue perusal of this note found in the pocket of a dress she had expressly forborne to've worn (the lavender) not even this shall, no no no no no.

[*indecipherable line*]

"Surprise" is but pique at one's inability to immediately assimilate the unforeseen. There is no magic to it.

"Come Smoke a Coca-Cola"
or: *The Musicality of the Times Explained*

A "Report from the Capsule"

One refuge was the thought that all was rhythm – as it must have been, given the incessant throbbing of the machine.

Which of us has not been moved by (the surviving) strophes of his "Ode to the Capsule," comparing the susurrus of the servomotors to the (imagined) rustle of the leaves in the wind – based upon *what*, I ask you, that Stakhanovite Act of Invention, based upon what but those stunningly purple passages, the "Chet's Boathouse" scene in *Newport Summer*, and the beating of his own heart?

His only other knowledge of periodicity was the mechanical – he who, of course, had never seen a sunset. And, yes, he wrote of the woods, and the "watch-bill of day-and-night," of the "'*égarements*' of the animals," creating (imagining) an outer world based on an inner, and who is to say which the larger?

"Come smoke a Coca-Cola," he wrote, with the dateline, as always, *In Ovo*.

And as we read we must remember that those allusions commonplace to us were, to him, subjects of mystery.

"Come smoke a Coca-Cola" giving rise to two volumes upon his (mis)understood knowledge of the Riots, which, who, who has not seen, has been left undiverted by his efforts to parse?

"Drink Ketchup Cigarettes" . . .

. . . but this concerns itself with rhythm, for which disquisition I must recur, once again, to the Capsule's "reading shelf," on which we find Buchalter's *Musicology for the Beginner*.

I will draw the reader's attention to its chapter on notation, page 1; in the margin, to the left of the subhead, "Drawing the Staves," we find, in his hand, "Like the beat beat of the tom-toms," and that 'pointing hand' symbol (☞), directing our attention to the facing page, and his essay, "Hatikvah, Imber, and Al Jolson's 'Anniversary Song.'"

Was it an ignorance of orthography, a defaced line of type? What was it to've caused him to misunderstand the line "Could we but recall that sweet moment sublime?" and to've given rise to his essay, "Who was Wee-Butt?"?[1]

1 – May it not be understood as ironic, i.e., as referring, as in schoolyard humor, to its *inverse*: e.g. large chaps called "Shorty"; fat ones, "Slim"; and "Wee-Butt", then, a cognomen of the steatopygian?[A]

A – Cf.
FELLOW A: Hi there, "Crisco!"
FELLOW B: Why do you call me "Crisco?"
FELLOW A: "Fat-in-the-can!" [A1]

A1 – See also *Weebut in Earthquake Land.*

We now proceed from the confusing to the arbitrary.

EPICTETUS, *WHO'S MINDING THE STOA?*[1]

1 –

QUESTION: What is the difference, and why characterize one as one rather than the other?

ANSWER: In the second we see the absence of hope.

QUESTION (THE WRANGLER): Do we not, however, also there perceive the birth of salubrious resignation?

JANE OF TRENT

The Wobbly

Let Us Consider the "Wobbly"
or: *An Early Connection to "Cola"*

Gone off to meet Joe Hill,
Gone off to meet Joe Hill.
Worked my life worried, and I'm worried still.
Gone off to meet Joe Hill.
'SONG OF THE WOBBLY HUNG FROM THE BRIDGE'

This verse is, unfortunately, all that survives of the original. And speculation on the identity of the "Wobbly" has, therefore, been based (until now) upon and only upon those facts im- and explicit in the verse itself:

1. That the Wobbly is going off to meet Joe Hill;
2. That the Wobbly has spent his or her life "worried";
3. That he or she is still worried;
4. That he or she was hung from a bridge;
5. That he or she sang.

Bridge hanging was, of course, a form of lynching or impromptu capital punishment. Popular as not requiring the (seemingly endless) tedium of judicial procedure, *lynching* flourished up to the twentieth century, and enjoyed a brief subsequent popularity during the time of the Riots.

Now, what might the Wobbly have done to bring this "lynching" down on him- or herself.*[1]

1 – Who is to say the Wobbly was human? Might it not have been a bird, or an ape (cf. the works of Edmund Lear), or as is found (much too) frequently in children's literature, a totally confected creature?

Yes, might an ape (to choose my favorite) not have hung from a bridge? Might not a sloth, a snake, a bat?

The question why any of the above might have been "worried" could have been so easily decided (as might the identity of the Wobbly) from context, had the subsequent verses survived. But there is no use crying over spilt milk.

---

* Or itself.

We don't know.[2]

We know only "this is a mystery," as the ancient religious wrote. "It is a mystery." But is there not, in this, an odd comfort . . .? To be able to "identify" the unknown, to negotiate the transition from terror to consternation, which is the essential work of society?[3]

One school, then, holds (we must say conveniently) that "it is a mystery." And then, there is the "anecdotal" tradition, which confutes the Wobbly with the Toll Hound.

Was it because the Toll Hound danced?[4] Was the tradition based upon the merest association of "dance" and gyration ("wobbling")?

Might the Toll Hound have hung from a bridge?

Might the Toll Hound have been "worried"?

May we consider[5] dancing *work*?

Who was Joe Hill?

I refer here to the monumental *Surtees and the Hunting Life* by A. Bassett: ". . . neither can we ignore the possibility that 'Joe Hill' was a corruption of 'John Peel', that imaginary[6] master of foxhounds" –

D'ye ken John Peel, with his coat so gay
D'ye ken John Peel at the break of day
D'ye ken John Peel, when he's far far away
W'his hound and his horns in the morning.

Might we not suggest that the Hound was "gone," to *a* "Hill" – the *personification* of a hill, that the Hound was, then, "gone hunting"; and

2 – Ginger, of course, knew. For the verse was glued, as we know, to the wall of her cell.
3 – Cf. W. and A. Durand, *The Life History of Civilization* – "either a work of overwhelming invention or a vast pile of shit" (*New York Times*).
4 – On the precise steps executed by the Toll Hound, we suggest *Labanotation and The Heritage of Petipa*, or *Found in a Trunk in Pinsk.*[A]
5 – Or consider that the Toll Hound considered.
6 – But was "John Peel" imaginary? Cf. David Ogilvy, "John Peel and Ciquita Banana," *Advertising Age*, December 1961.

A – Scratched on a (beaverboard) partition between two commodes, Institute of Slav Studies, Balliol:

QUESTION: What's the wallpaper at the Ipatiev House?

ANSWER: Holey holey holey.

See also *A Cottage Small by a Waterfall* and *The Parking Meter Problem: Rainy Day Fun for Shut-Ins.*

that a later time, ignorant of that MFH, of fox hunting, of foxes, of gentility and grace, of everything, in short, corrupted "John Peel" into "Joe Hill" and, thence, into nothing?[7]

Mrs. Bassett does not address – indeed the work is neither intended to address, nor would it be an appropriate vehicle in which to address – the issue of *culpability*, i.e. *why* was the Toll Hound hung?

But I will advert (and future scholarship must try the case) that there is worth in the pursuit of the connection between the Hound and the Cola Riots.

Musicologists may consider the *virtual identity* of the song "John Peel" and the twentieth-century jingle "Pepsi Cola hits the spot" (1950–60, and resurfacing, of course, as "The Song of the Republicans" during the early days of the Riots).

7 – "A. Bassett, what a dyspeptic bitch . . .", "Talk of the Town," *New Yorker*, date unknown.

"Like Shrimps that Crash in the Night . . ."
From the original *Errata*

If you put enough monkeys at enough typewriters, sooner or later they will bash out promotional material for a pharmaceutical concern.

There is no help for it. It is an ongoing process. All the king's horses or all of their men[1] cannot deter them. Nor can they accelerate the process. They can only "stand by," some with their cigarettes, some with their oats, and wait upon the pleasure of their betters.

1 – This is, of course, a vast mis-statement of the problem. The "men," in the original, are the *king*'s men. This rendition suggests the men owe their allegiance/service to the *horses*! It was upon such a syntactical solecism, of course, that hung the fate of the Martian Dragoons "that day." [A, B]

A – John C. ("Jolly") Rogers, Reg. Sgt-Major, U.M.D. (Ret.), *Ruffles and Flourishes: My Years on Mars*. See also his *Trooping the Colour, and the Colour's Always Red* and *The Woman in Me.*
B – The misconstruction of the possessive pronoun surfaces once again as revelatory in the Toll Hound saga: "And Bingo was his name–o". How often do we find relief in the picayune? In the overlooked and misunderstood, in the misfiled, nay, in the very *vespasienne* whose discovery retransforms into a charming Parisian street corner, an operative outpost of hell.

A Poem

A Poem[1]

They say that Bennigsen
in propria persona
Never habited the Capsule.
Infamia, they scream,
and *Fraud.*
Their screams
Are music to our Jaded Ears.

O, Ears. Most outboard of appendages.
Who praises thee?
(Yes, this or that aurally fixated swain,
Be-smitten of the Lobes. But *otherwise*?
Oh, please.

And what *is* Poetry?
Or Truth . . .?
But the rain, Beating on my . . .)
    et cetera

1 – How odd are the "works of the past." How, to our eyes, "quaint," as if (and further investigation may, in fact, establish this to've been the case) it existed merely as a "foil," a Sancho to our Don Quixote,[A] a relief, or "ground," to our impressive "figure."

It is this *aperçu* which colors much or both of the true and of the pseudo-scholarship, and work of reconstruction of the Time Before the Riots, and which informs much of the speculation about Greind.

A – Miguel de Cervantes, *Don Quixote.*

end of section one

The Library

The Library
In which the investigation turns from the quest for information *per se*, to perigrinations on its transmission.

What of that bloke who burned the Library in Alexandria, Virginia – the Library or the Stop 'n' Shop?[1]

How must he have felt, could he have realized that his deed, too, would and must be forgotten?

A list of names in which his *may* have been found – the catalogue card (discarded) in *Moving Picture Boys in Earthquake Land*, The Humphries Memorial Library, Alexandria, Virginia, shows four removals in the years 1951–75. It has been remarked that as the stacks were open, anyone could have removed the volume at any time and simply "taken it home."

They could, additionally, have simply (and legally) taken the book down from the shelf and sat at one of the solid oak tables we are

1 – The Stop 'n' Shop paradigm in Bill Gapes, *The Destruction of All Knowledge*, vol. XII (Punchboard Press, Twenty-nine Palms, Sector Four, Group Four, New South Mars), with a tip of the Hatlo Hat to the Grinian Asteroids and All the Ships at Sea: BUT WHAT IF THE GUY FROM THE SHOE DEPARTMENT BURNT IT DOWN?[A]

And also:

Abie had a Candystore
Business going bad.

from *The Protocols of the Elders of Zion*, Burbank.

A – But what if the guy from the shoe department burnt/burned it down? Who would have blamt/blamed him? Think about it. Sitting there, sniffing old fat ladies' feet, trying to cram them in, a size too small. Who would of blamed him, cause* what did the whole thing† mean to him, any case? "Get up, go to work, sniff old ladies' feet, go home, try not to think about it." I would of burnt it down, that case, anyone would. So would *you*!!

Cf. Bennigsen:

This sty, this shithole of a world
this worse-than-obscene compilation
of all cruelties
in which what higher good than
[*indecipherable*].

See also the works of Greind (Bennigsen) and *How He Came Down the Chimney*.

* For. † The universe.

sure we wish the Library to've possessed, and there, in a moment of distraction or inattention (or *absence*) on the part of the Librarian, scribbled in the book those words which indicate to us its (possible) presence in the hands of the incendiary: "I want to burn this shithole down."

But can we think that the malefactor saw fit to inscribe his name and intention in a book leaving what even the merest pyro-criminologist must surely understand as a "clue"?

Why would a fellow do that?

Well, an ordinary thief, a rapist, public official, sodomite, sophisticator of beer, war criminal, etc., one who, in short, looked to enjoyment with impunity as the *sine qua non* of a successful outing of his particular freak, such a one would not, it is true, choose to advertise.

But is it not in the nature of the incendiary, of the arsonist, to, perhaps, *wish* to have credit for his deed? And if not of the arsonist, then, of this *particular* arsonist, who, we know, torched the joint *specifically* to get the credit?

"They can stuff the volumes in, but who will be remembered longer, them or me, who burnt the joint down?" he[2] is recorded to've said.

Well, anybody who believes in "Last Requests" is missing the whole point of being dead.[3]

But this gent thought it good to torch the repository of learning, to take upon himself that office usually reserved for history (wars, floods, volcanoes, things of that nature) and to strive for immortality through an act of eradication – his (presumed) suicide, his (certain) disappearance giving rise to that contemporary hit single, "You can only be immortal during your lifetime," which anecdotal evidence identifies (one must say, not without weight) as the (at that time) State Song of Indiana.

2 – "He" being, of course, as per above, either Bruce Wallingford, Dora Jessica Butz, Sally James, or Deanna Marcodeangelo; see *Annals of the Humphries Memorial Library*, transferred from the original card catalogue to microfiche, 1991; to DAT, 1999; again to paper, 2032; and lost in the Cola Riots, surviving (in part) as a remnant, in the New Federal Document Retrieval Museum ("Playland"), Fentervale, Falls Church, Virginia ("Children Welcome, Absolutely No Pets, Homosexuals Preferred, No Shoes, No Shirt, No Service").

3 – Rabbi Larry Kushner, Sudbury, Massachusetts, 1996.

But to return. His act seems to've had a lasting influence upon Greind (Bennigsen) who alludes (how slyly!) to it in his suicide note,[4] in which he writes:

Helen of Troy
The Library in Alexandria
Napoleon
. . . what's the use?

Why do I employ the adverb "slyly"? Because he knew what the "use" was, or else he wouldn't have written. He would have shot himself.[5]

And why the Library, rather than the Stop 'n' Shop? Because, gentle Reader, good Reader, Reader so ready and moist, Reader so [. . .],[6] we just don't know.

It *could* have been one of the four, bent on the eradication of all knowledge.[7] It could have been a disaffected clerk, or manager, or customer, put off by the "mood music"; or a young, say a young couple, sneaking in after the store had closed to make love in the aisles, and drink wine, and, perhaps, to light a can of Sterno™ "Liquid Heat" to enhance the experience, their bodies picked out in the half-dark,[8] who, perhaps, "knocked over" the can in their fumblings, and, perhaps, it burnt the grocery store down, and *spread* to the Library next door, eradicating all knowledge.

It *could* have happened that way. Who's to say?

4 – We here use, and will always use, the phrase as it is used in general conversation to refer to the *first* note. We have no patience with the quibbler – those academics and shitheads who've based their careers upon the mountains of monographs differentiating between the taxonomy "Note 1," "Note 2," 'Note 3," and those plumping for "The Note," "The Note in the Garden," "Bubba's Note," "The Coffee Stain," etc. What a *waste* of time . . .
5 – Granted, he *did*, eventually, shoot himself, but [*indecipherable*].
6 – Expurgated.
7 – *Was* it knowledge, though, or was it merely "information" – that lifeless, boring stuff the schoolmasters had been trying to cram down our throats these last five million years? No *wonder* they were taken out and killed.*
8 – We are assuming the light would have been left on in the dairy case. Why? Because it makes a pretty picture.

* Good job.

Let Us Cast Our Attention, Then, to "Upheavals of the Great"
In which the reader is exposed to another acrostic

. . . the death of Bennigsen, the suicide of Kennedy, the lone anguish of Edith Wilson, caught in a loveless marriage, and unable to communicate save by notes scribbled both in invisible ink and code,[1] and thrown to the mercy of chance and an uninterested public, falling past the Museum on their way to the floor of the Factory.

Which of us has not been moved at the thought, and, yes, at the sight of the lone surviving note, writ upon the back of a packing slip in her own urine, which when viewed under ultraviolet light reveals:

R A S S
D F J J
D A S S

1 – Cf. *Us and Them* by Martin Buber:

. . . an ancient rune or cuneiform, from which modern science can render only this phrase: "We can deal with the *Goyim* – God help us with the German Jews" – its meaning, if, indeed, it has one, lost in the mists of time.[A]

And was not Krautz to posit his own "secret writing," as it were – a Harmonics of Behavior, in which, given the tonic, one could deduce the changes: mediant, submediant, dominant, subdominant, tonic; all behavior marching, orderly, toward home, like an old tomcat, set in his ways, upon his midnight walk – his very diversion – here to urinate, here to frolic with a compliant female, thence to the garbage pails of a restaurant – an old tomcat, I say, whose very diversions and seeming pointless anfractuosities reveal, upon some observation, a routine ordered to the last degree? Would that it were, and, gentle Reader, may I be pardoned my *obiter dictum* on the Human State, but what, finally, is the end of all our labors, and what the reduction of all effort if not understanding of (in an attempt to better) our state?

But any theory, however serviceable, may be stretched past the (elastic, yes, in some cases, but finite, in all) point of utility.

A – Quoted by Krautz (ibid.) and I may take this as a happy time to peregrinate and offer that reminder "nothing is such a sure prognostication of a second-class mind as a facility with languages."

The letters so mellifluous, so suggestive; the code, of course, never broken, and, when discovered, employed as a justification for her further imprisonment.

Is it not ironic that we today know less of the state of her mind at that time than of the percentage of albumen and undissolved solids in her urine?[2]

"D F J J," indeed.

And how the history of that time might have been altered could her heroic, nay, Stakhanovite efforts to communicate have met with success?

How fickle a public, how harsh a time – to change from the adulation, nay, the ecstasy of the pickerpape parade on her return, to the moral, mental and physical oubliette of the barred powder room of the Museum Lobby –

. . . that scene, treated so often in song and fable, in film, mural, and – the highest endorsement of its consonance to our contemporary lot – in pastiche. This scene:

The blind, deaf widow in the powder room – charged with the captaincy of this great nation, and reduced to writing on the packing slip of what contemporary research must identify as a window frame, reduced to scribbling nonsense in piss and throwing it out of the window – this hero, this saint . . .

Et cetera.

2 – See also O. Neselrod, *Urine Testing in Literature*, and the companion volume, *Bend Over and Spread 'Em.*[B]

B – The one aspect of the situation not examined, either at the time or later (to my knowledge) is that of the *container*. Who has examined it?* What *held* the urine? Please see, Percy Bysshe Shelley, "I Made It Out of Clay" and "The Cadence Count of the Fourteenth Martian Dragoons (Mech.)":

A Traveler in an Antique Land
One, Two, Three, Four
Came on a Statue in the Sand
Jody called your gal a whore
Sound off . . .

* Presumably the FBI.

The Papers on the Shelf
In which the investigation subtly shifts to a perusal of the Capsule[1]

The Settlement of Michigan
Birnam Wood
The Strikeplate
The Amulet (*disputed*)

1 – "For this is but another way to know him – to know what he read or ate" (*Wisdom of the Fantasist*).

The Settlement of Michigan

The Settlement of Michigan

Bruce "Wild Man" Muskie, *New England Journal of Medicine*, Fall 2049[1]

Survival of Indian Voyageur Symbiology[2] in the Myth of the Grande-Pacquards

The fragment begins: ". . . and a tattoo which read, 'My other car is a Rolls-Royce.'"

His eyes bulged with what may have been fear or a wry surprise at the finality of it all – as if it were a drama or a novel whose sad ending is known, but whose narrative is so enchanting that one approaches it with, none the less, that hope that somehow, *this time . . .*

. . . his eyes, I say, bulged with what we may call surprise. Perhaps we could call it "welcome."

Was it not fitting, would it not be fitting to call it so, as he himself had written,

Anger, in business dealings, is a veil between you and the customer – yes, you may be wroth, you may have *been* deluded, cheated, mistreated in every possible way, *and yet*, is it still upon you *to close the sale.*

If not, move on to your next appointment. If so, know it's your anger which prohibits you from doing so. Not the customer, no, for it is not his "job" to buy from you. It is your job to sell, and, as we saw in Step 6, recognition of responsibility is the key to the top half of the pyramid.

What are our tools, for Step 6 upward? Let's review:

1 – I call the reader's attention, as if such prompting were required, to the "Drearest/ Dearest" parapraxis in the letter to Goessals, "Drearest Friend."[A]

2 – Cf. Nathaniel Hawthorne, "One Little Letter (and the Letter is 'U'): The Difference Between a Champ and a Chump" (18??).

A – "A Man, a Plan, a Canal: Suez", *Psychotherapy in Civil Engineering*, 19??, and the wealth of obbligati thereupon, e.g., Dearest Fiend, Drearest Feint, Nearest Friend, etc. Now this, certainly, is immortality of a sort – to've added a phrase to the language is to've touched the Community Cortex deeper and more finally than praise or riches or rewards could testify. It is, in *fact*, "twice blest, in that it blesseth him that gives and her that gives" (Germaine Greer, *Spotty*).

Birnam Wood Do Come to Dunsinane
or: *Cheezit, the Copse*

Alarmism and Millenniumism in Late Twentieth-Century America

One cannot invest too much effort, it would seem, given the spate of theses, tracts, broadsheets – but I will not bore (with the blessing) with yet another catalogue, falling the victim, thus, of that grave error of the climber, perched upon the highest crag, moved by the urge to fly, who flings himself down, attempting to still by surrender, that tropism he found, if the truth were known, and the question could be put to him as he falls, in the end, less irksome than the prospect of that death, so imminent, on the rocks of whatever the chance composition of the base of that protuberance below.

Unlike, then, that man, rendered unhappy by the search for happiness, I will not (once again, *deo volonte*) in submission to that urge for closure, commit that irremediable error of undoing, of gainsaying, of betraying the *essence* of my quest.

(In the mountaineer or climber, *height*, in these peregrinations, *clarity*.)

"Wolf, wolf!" the boy cried. And there was no wolf.

Later, the tale informs us, there was a wolf. And the boy continued to cry. But, we are told, "his cries went unheeded." And the wolf devoured him.

Might one not say (certainly not *in extremis*, *vis-à-vis* that wild beast, but, here, in safety and repose, understanding the tale as a parable, which, for good or ill, we must allow it to be), might one not, then, say, that the *good* which the boy pursued (and he must have, must he not, have deemed it good indeed, as he knew that the ability to command his listeners' attention/concern diminished) might and must one not say that it was their *attention* which he craved. And that the potential to command their *protection* using the same formula ("Wolf") is but coincidental – that the boy had had all the good he could derive from his operations, that the unwillingness of the villagers to run to him at the time of his *actual* attack by a wolf is notable only within the parable – that in the less specialized operations of real life, it was and would have been the villagers' responsibility to run to the boy *each* time he cried "wolf," *ad infinitum*, to ensure his amendment, to move away, or to have him killed?

Similarly, the boy: had he had it in his view not to "round out the story," but to save his own life, would he not have been better put to've shouted something different? ("Fire," for example, or "Rape," or "Look, I have found gold!")

I think some short reflection must compel agreement.

The Strikeplate[1]

> As feast, famine, so must form perennially pursue function. "Male and Female created them (s)he." And, as the female to the male, so to the bolt itself the strikeplate; and, so, then, its necessary form.
>
> *AN IDEOGRAPHY OF THE RECEPTIVE*, op. cit.

It needs no apologia, nor will I embark upon one here (what could one gain?). That era of the phrase so unaccountably unremarkable to the mind of the times – Architectural (or "Structural"): Reconstructionism.

It has been (re-)established, licensed, ever, until – we would say "the end of time," but reasonable historical wisdom might say better "until superseded by folly or fashion." The Reconstructionists held as the single indubitable fact of life this: Form must (should) follow function.[2]

We say of any thing, "It was better when it was small," and, yet, we burn to make it large.

But the strikeplate must lie in proportion to the bolt. And elaboration of the form outside the confines of the jamb must lead to at least the possibility of purchase by the malefactor, such elaboration falling into and under the taint not only, thus, of supererogation, but of outright defeat of the prime (stated) purpose (of the object)

[corrupt]

1 –
QUESTION (As the students had it, "in those days") Why is "The Strikeplate" included?
ANSWER Shut up and deal.[A]

2 – Greind himself was once asked, "Must form follow function?", to which he replied, "Surest thing you know."

A – Alternatively:
1 Shut up in Deal – *et seq.*: Derry, Lobb, Concairn, etc.
2 Shut up, indeed.

The Amulet
[*disputed*]

The Amulet

Found on the remnant of flyleaf of The Dust Jacket – its heading (reconstructed): "For a sample of a similar work we think you'd enjoy, read on!"

"I once worked in a smoked salmon factory," he said.

She understood him to mean that he was, therefore, about to order something other than the fish.

But he went on.

"At that time I met a most interesting man."

Now, Ginger's only interest at this time and place was food. But she lowered the menu politely and prepared to be bored out of her cotton bloomers.

"Oh, the lengths they go to," she thought. "If they'd only say, 'Hey, *Miss* . . .' or 'Babe,' or 'Bitch,' or 'Ma'am,' or, ''Scuse me, how about a round or so of "*you* know"?'" But, no . . .

"*This* is the Woman's curse," she thought, "and, if there was Original Sin and it had something to do with eating the apple, then the *punishment* is not childbirth, it is not menstruation, it is having to listen to some jerk trying to get laid."

". . . the *good* cholesterol," the man was saying. She nodded.

". . . and he said he'd come from Mars." Her ears perked up.

"The *planet*?" she said.

He nodded. "Yup."

"*Huh*," she said.

". . . but *you* don't want to hear this." Ginger shrugged.

"How lonely it is to be lonely and to have no one to be lonely with," she thought.

"Or, to have no one with whom to be lonely."

"Those days," she thought, "those long-gone days on the farm. Those long-ago days. Those days of . . ."

When she looked up from the table the place was closed, the lights doused, the chairs put up on the tables, her coffee long gone cold, and her companion dead.

She searched for the check, and found there was none.

"Well, that's thoughtful," she thought. "But what a crock. 'Fish factory.' 'F it had been true, wouldn't he have said a 'smokery,' or a 'fish'ry?' I think he was only trine to get over on me, 'ndit would have been *so much* the simpler to've said so."

She reached down to pat her companion on the head, and spied around his neck the chain, and, at the end of the chain, hung down, resting on the table, the Amulet.

"Aha. *That*'s where you are, you little sucker," she thought. "Wonders never *cease*."

We do not, of course, see the Amulet again until "The Trial of Dick and Jane"[1] and it is this *lacuna* to which this monograph must now direct its efforts.

What, in short, happened to the Amulet?

We are not the first to ask this question, but we are the first to utter it as the purely rhetorical prolegomenon you, dear Reader, happy Reader, are about to discover it to be. *The Amulet was there all the time.*

It is not, it will not be found, I assure you, remiss or supererogatory to, as it were, "back and fill" – to give those unacquainted with the Canon the, I promise you, few (and, those, painlessly acquired) tools necessary to construct that theoretical underpinning, or *Grundisse* without which the, if I may, convoluted beauty of the proposition cannot be appreciated.

The essence of the form, of course, is that of *The Search.* It has been revealed elsewhere that the significance of *Mars*, both *in ipso* and as a symbol – as a symbol both plastic and verbal[2] – and, then, by extension, of the *Amulet* resided in this: it was *red.*

Now, what might that other "red thing" be, that thing which the first might be taken to symbolize, if not this: the *Grail*, the Holy Grail?[3]

And why was the Grail red? What, finally, *was* that *shallow red cup*, that cup full of (holy) blood, for which the troubadours, their instruments aloft, searched?

1 – See *Dickin' Jane: The Hidden Life of Edgar Rice Burroughs*, op. cit.
2 – For a discussion of the (possible) (virtual) interchangeability of the two, please see Brunner, Feld, et al., *It All Ends Up the Same Place.*
3 – See Vondervogelveider, Wagner, et al.

It was there all the time.

It was as close as the object of the salmon salesman's desire, it was right across the table, it was in the skies, it hung around his neck and it could be seen (or inferred) on any street corner in the world.

[. . .][4]

Now, on to the "symbol."

It has long been an article of faith that the faint outline pressed (or etched or extruded) into the Sphere was either random – a (to beg the question) naturally occurring blot, or "foxing," the result of age or perhaps of imperfection in the "manufacture process" – or was an abstracted, which is to say, "simplified" or inexpert attempt to render the outline of Malathusa County, California.

A third choice exists. It has always been understood that Greind of course meant to indicate that it was possible to take it for a *representation* of a dog.

And we can but wish for the eventual evolution or return of humanity to a state possessed of sufficient calm and reason never to give rise to such loathsome, such obscene and godless rubbish as the libel that "he said it was a dog," and the like – the foolish and always arrogant, nay, invariably fascist attempts of the deranged to leach all meaning from words, and reduce all human intercourse to struggles with the blunt and the sharp.

4 – The monograph here continues on the congruity of the Grail and the Amulet. As it offers nothing either in addition to nor more interesting or supportable than its reduction in the opening paragraphs, it is omitted.

It has become *de rigueur* to remind, at this point, that it has never been established that "The Papers on the Shelf" were actually *on* the shelf, or, for that matter, "in the Bookcase."

That they were discovered in the Capsule is, of course, a matter of "common knowledge," and, thus, subject to the doubt only of the philosopher, historian, or hobbyist.

Section Two

The Sample Paragraph
from *Tales of the Joke Code*[1]

He was a dog. But he was a *happy* dog. There was no other word to describe it. At least not to *Billy's* mind!

For it was the grin on Chipper's face that began Billy's day – the wet, sloppy kisses, the excited wagging of the tail, the expression which said, better than words, "Let's go!" – this was the "break fast" that Billy loved best.

Connect the pronouns in the paragraph above to reveal a secret sign, letter, or numeral. Your next clue will be found in next month's issue. Arrange the clues to form a sentence or instruction.[2]

1 – *Bongazine* (February–July 2101), © the editors.[A]
2 – It was Cohen, of course, who, not recognizing "that" as a pronoun, reduced a sketch which should have been the letter K into an H, and therefore misunderstood the Old Wrangler's message, "BE KIND" as "BEHIND."

A – Misfiled here during "Phase Two" of the Riots, its "courtesy" placement has offered, if not inspiration, at least hope, to a, granted, ever-decreasing number of academics.

If this, then that
A recurrence to the Epitaph, and, thus, to the Mall

And, if this, then that. Or, if this,
why not, then, that?

The above stands, perhaps, as the single, as the singular, instance of a *bon mot*, recorded at death,* *wherein* the accuracy of the phrase is absolutely certain, but its utterer's identity completely problematic. For we know, do we not, of the "din in the Lazarette"; and, yes, we know of the "distraction of the Nurse,"

For, when she turned around, she could not say
"for sure" which of the three had uttered it – and now,
she saw, too clearly, "all of them are dead."

As was (and is) the redactor. And do we not, then, "aping Gibbon,"† declare: "Then was the time of the compilers, of the editors, and of the anthology." Yes. We do, but what choice have we, who dwell in this cosmic shitstorm of *sensoria*, of information, of both "truth and blather intermixed?"[1] Yes.

Yes, wherein the central question must send the observant/meditative nature, if not "round the bend," at least to that point sufficient to let him o'erlook it.

Pad your room, then, furtive creatures all, wherein it will not avail to side with the warders, for, as they said in the Riots, "they have voted with their feet."

We do not know who screamed the Epitaph – which of the "Three who Died." We do not know who graved it on the Plinth upon the Mall, we take on faith the chamber's occupant, and we call that faith "reason." No, not reason, which would suggest (whatever its defensibility) an element of election, which is to say, at the least, an operation of the processes of *doubt*; no, but *knowledge*, which is to say blind and immutable acceptance.

1 – Maltz, Buck and Kreutzer, *Bongazine Forever*.

* Generally termed "last words," "dying utterance," etc. † Ha ha.

"Pad your rooms and eat the buttons off the wall" – so wrote the Mystic,[2] he who devoted his life to establishment of the Authorship of the Poem, and he who rose to wealth and fame "smoothing out the wrinkles in the silver foil." What is it but error?

The first Commentators died for their intractability, and went to the Plinth "a-smilin'."

How it must enervate, how it depresses one to feel that their self-satisfaction, that their repletion, that their sense of purpose would in no wise have been diminished had they lived to discover, beyond any doubt, that their information was flawed, their precepts, so derived, therefore absurd, that they, in short, had lived and died in error.

On the other hand, what the hell – it kept them out of trouble.

2 – Paul P. Crumble, *My Life in Advertising* (Bogside Press, 20??). Cf. The Twelfth Sermon of the Fantasist: "This year I'm going to the mountains."

Time

Time
An *obiter dictum* upon that which "is passing."

> Get dressed, you married gentlemen; or, "If Your Wife is Frigid, Freeze her Till she Burns to Thaw."
> From: *400 PIECES OF A SCARY RIDE*

The Bible – no, we will not say "bible," for would we then imply we mean to have the term accepted as meaning Koran, Torah, whatever-the-hell, Joke Code, Panishads and Sutras, and so on and so on? Or would it mean we mean to exclude them? How can we determine which?

And would that determination, or its attempt, not consume that which is least replaceable: time?

It has been argued that life itself is less replaceable than time. But this, I feel, simply begs the question. The question in this case being, "What is Time without life?"

Thus we perceive Time has no meaning without life.

A-ha, you say, do you mean to state that the eons and ages between the slime-mold or the too-long-left hunk of cheese, or whatever it was which gave rise to that first mold, or spore which grew (how slowly!) into what we come to know as ourselves – do you mean to say that that period has no meaning, as it was empty of intellectual life, of life sufficiently sentient to note the passage of Time?

Or might you say (if I've correctly gauged your mood) that the disprobative period you propose predates even that, that you mean to indicate that time, say, from the start of the whole thing – whatever that means to you – that time of nothingness, or before-being – that time, in short, so far removed from our own in every particular that you are powerless to conceive of it and must employ a primitive, a mythologic construct to do so, i.e., "that time before everything was," "that time when dogs could speak," etc.

Do you mean to adopt, I say, then, for your benchmark, that period commencing then, and running to the appearance of this traduced and violated shithole of a planet, and say to me of it,* "Do you mean to imply there was no Time, then, as there was no life?" And to continue, "A-ha, then, there I have you! For although there was no life, there now is life, and I who am now alive exercise my right of marshaling perception into expression, if you will, to cast my gaze back and exclaim, 'That time I speak of was a long, long time'?"

I will address your question.

One. The period of which you speak as encompassing "a long, long time" is incapable of measurement. You adopt, as I have above suggested, the crutch of a mythologic construct to express "a time I cannot imagine." And do thus disqualify yourself (I think you would agree) as any do, as *all* do in a scientific dispute who revert to special pleading.

You do not say "a year," or "a decade," etc., as you cannot. As you are lost and call, as does a helpless child, as does an egoless adult, on your very adversary to assist you.

Two. I did not, in the first instance, saying time was nothing without life, mean to engender this notional, and, finally, bootless discussion involving metaphysics, myth, and history, no. It was my intent to convey that my time, that *my* time is precious to me – that it seems to me to be quite all I have, and if I do not spend it happily, involved in this or that interesting examination, study (yes, even rumination), if, in short, I am *bored*, I would rather be dead.

The Bible, I say, that conjunction of ancient Semitic and somewhat less ancient Greek and Graeco-Semitic myths, laws, stories, legends, divine writ (perhaps) (which of us is to say?), parables, proverbs, and, in short, most any category of diversion and instruction mixed promiscuously in a manner and form which, if encountered in a modern work not enjoying the considerable benefit of its provenance and antiquity, would most likely be rejected *instanter* by all but the most curious of the unemployed, intellectual, or leisure class – the Bible, the Koran, the Torah, Sutras, Vedas, and myths of most every land (and it requires no scholarship to confirm what we feel instinctively: that each land, that each people, that each group, that each club, that each marriage must require a myth, and, having displayed it, live according to its precepts – or more likely fail to so live). (But who is to say? Perhaps

* This period.

there is that perfect land, that happy land, of joy – peopled by simple folk, living their pure lives of simplicity, subject to and content to subjugate themselves to a benign myth, which myth guards, instructs and comforts them? But I doubt it.)

The Bible (by which I mean to indicate all condign myths – or theologic compedia) instructs us to Love Our Neighbor.[1]

Thus let me round out my thesis, my, let me say, prolegomenon, for the bulk of my thesis must remain hid until the resolution of the appositeness, or the lack, of my first term. Or, better, let me discard it and start afresh, employing Occam's Razor, that best, that most applicable of friends, let me employ it not as an axiom of reasoning, no, but of action. And throw that which offends me to the winds.[2] And adopt in its stead a simpler, and, to use an analogy from scaffolding, a "steadier" base. I now set it aside and start anew.

1 – I do not mean to malign, and, in fact, abjure any intent to malign either here or elsewhere, any writ or scripture of any known or – if such there be – yet-to-be-discovered tribe, sect, or people which does not so instruct. Reflection reveals that I, no less than you, gentle Reader, am subject to ethnocentrism. I have taken one aspect of *my* myth, or *Weltanschauung*, and posited its universality, on no evidence save my subscription to it. Must there not be – yes, there must – those groups devoted to expulsion of their neighbors; and must there not exist monstrous great piles of records of the most grueling description, being the world myth or whatever mumbo-jumbo, of this or that tribe in which those outside the immediate, the most immediate bonds of communal or, mayhap, of consanguinal germanity are denoted "devils," the eradication of whom is denominated *summum bonum*?

Of course there must. And I will leave it to be argued elsewhere whether such division of the world into the moieties (us and them) does not engender a greater, a *greater* humanity. (Such, granted, within the limits of the tribe. A creation of that division, the Good, "us," and the Bad, "them." And I propose that even the more advanced sects make this division but are, perhaps, less aware of it.)

But perhaps I am full of shit.

2 – "If by chance the eye offends you, pluck it out, lad." (A. E. Houseman, *Journal of the British Ophthalmologic Association*, 20??)

Dear Diary
Source: The Diary[1]

How insipid those words seem. How incapable of rousing the least excitement or emotion in me, sparing always a self-pity.

How sad. And how far we have come since the Glory Days. What shall I do today? I think I shall die. I shall not write of the day-to-day, of the weather, nor of the shopping. Nor my weight, nor of those this notebook would require me to miss.

I do not miss them.

I wish that they were dead. The weather is overcast, as it has been, it seems to me, these years. It is not only my weight which disgusts, but my corporeal being of itself. I wish I were shut not of these last fourteen days, but of the lot of it. What must that make me? Dot dot dot dot. It is not, nor can it be, though it may be said, the now obvious results of the near completion of my most current round of experiments . . . No, it is my life, or let me say, "the short remainder," which has turned intolerable . . . Where have I mislaid that syringe . . .?

1 – Archives of the Commission. Search on: Capsule/Bookcase/[Shelf]/Diary/Mars.

A Doubt

How Funny

> Doubt being "either the beginning or the absence of wisdom." Its investigation cannot help but conduce either to happiness or rue.
>
> ATTRIBUTED TO KRAUTZ:
> *NOTES UPON JANE OF TRENT*

> How funny, finally, to be *oneself* – a thing separate from one's work, from one's "life," and, perhaps, even from one's thoughts – do I go too far?

The above, of course, caption of the famous cartoon, "Greind at the Museum."[1]

The cartoon requires neither description nor exegesis, and will be found on many a wall, locker door, upon the outside or inside of a notebook (perhaps one of *yours*), etc. – but I will draw the reader's attention to what I suspect will be a previously undetected aspect of the piece: to the lower right-hand corner and the mound of "pebbles" (blurred or omitted in many or most of the late-generation reproductions). Magnification of a degree possible with good home-quality instruments reveals one of these pebbles to be, in fact, a pumpkin; or, to say more true, a jack-o'-lantern. Its face is carved as a historic figure, and that figure is Wilson.

In the original we see a *finesse* of detail and feeling all the more surprising in contrast with the quick, even blunt tone of the cartoon *toute entière* – the drawn and hollow cheeks, the distrait gaze, the eyeglasses, the thinning hair, the overall impression of anxiety, of care, of illness far outstrip the most healthy imagination's ability to encompass the notion of the possibility of true art on a pumpkin; and, on the other hand, "Why not?" We read and we denominate misguided those twentieth-century souls creating "art" out of the shredded laundry list found in the lint trap of their clothing driers. But are their operations

1 – *Bombazine*, 20??.

more risible, less worthy of respect, than the Buddhist or Hindu monks fashioning this or that image of devotion out of rancid butter?[2]

Granted, a painting or sculpture is of a greater potential permanence, but is not all (and, perhaps, this is the message of the butter) subject to the will of God?

The Ancients, in their fog, fashioned a bull calf out of gold.

Similarly misguided Italians, in another time, daubed paints upon stretched canvas, or hacked out a figure in marble or other soft stone.

Might not the pumpkin *rather than the image graven thereupon* be the hidden message of the cartoon's creator? Might it not?[3]

2 – Ghee.

3 – Subsequent discovery of the following month's (December's) issue shows the jack-o'-lantern replaced with the head of Kris Kringle, thus smashing into flinders the theorem above. Krautz (*fils*), expected to retire in ignominy from the discussion, to resign both his claim to the issue and his position at the University, stunned the (granted, starved-for-diversion) academic world with the publication of the unabashed and, frankly aggressive "Oh boo, oh hoo."[A] I quote, with permission:

Yah yah yah yah. I'm rubber, and you're glue. Everything you say bounces off me and sticks to you. Your mother is a whore. Blow me.

A – *Bombazine*, vol. 12, no. 5 (2021).

Obsess

For how can we comprehend the whole without an understanding of the parks?
OLMSTEAD

. . . he would obsess about Bennigsen's reputation as having been able, with one sweep of his arm, to draw a perfect circle.

He was, therefore, relieved beyond reason on discovering that the Earth itself was not perfectly round,* but, in effect, pear-shaped.

Further reflection, in fact, suggested to him, however, that, this being true, space did possess – in opposition to everything he had learned and come to accept *but not in opposition to his "senses"* – an "up" and "down."

"One plugs one hole," he wrote, "and, happy for less time than it takes the thought to form, discovers another one opening."[1]

Did this suggest to him a closed, hydraulic system?[2]

And, if so, of what? Of space? Of knowledge? Of the universe?

And might we not approach nearer to an understanding of his nature by answering *this* question, rather than the (seemingly more important) sequel: "How does this system operate?"

1 – "For if there is *up*, if there is *down*, must it not all, at some point, 'resolve,' or is that not, and must it not be, an illusion? Doors within doors! *Doors within doors!*" Two hundred years of scholarship accepted, without (in a unanimous display of respect) comment, that Bennigsen means "doors *beyond* doors." This lack of comment persisted until the publication in 2122 of Rinaldi's *Bennigsen and the Dutch Door*, wherein the subject's Low German antecedents were suggested as a possible explanation for what, otherwise, must have been taken (comment or not) as a solecism. As that can of worms has been (long) opened, I make fair to point out that, had he been alluding to Dutch architecture, he would have said, "Doors *above* (or *below*) doors." Confute me who can.[A]

2 – F. X. Bumphrey, Sacristan, St Catherine's Church (1931–81), *I Cover the Waterfont.*

A – See also, "The Pet Door," p. 307.

* Spherical.†

† Neither, of course, was it perfectly round. The editor's note was an impertinence.

The argument has here degenerated and it is at this point that "The Scholars of Old" traditionally stopped to sample "such viands as the hospitable were wont to place before those worthies."*

* i.e. *Whippies.*

Bongazine

Bongazine
Where, refreshed, we begin again.

Now let us recur to the use of "magazine," as you knew that we would – O gentle Reader, full of patience, full of wit, full of forbearance,* full of grace and worthy, finally, of emulation. For who would not wish to be as you – so replete with excellence, as if three readers were stuffed into a two-reader bag.[1]

O, good, oh yummy reader, reader of my dreams, how I would love to συνουσιασθοῦμε until the cows come home.

And then go out for tea.[2]

I'd like to thank you, and I'd like to spank you. But I do not have the time, and, so, I must recur, as I said, to the use of "magazine."

Now, anyone who's read a British novel of the Georgian Age will recall the first time he or she came acros(t) *goal* standing in for *gaol*, and hurried to the footnotes. No, it was not, you then found, a printer's error. No, no. That was how they talked back then. And, over time, one thing became the other. Just as friendship blossoms, now and then, into love, or love decays into indifference, or, unfortunately, into loathing, or . . . but you get my drift.

The phenomenon to which I here make bold, good gentle Reader, Reader kind, Reader possessed of everything, in short, which would induce a man to leave his hearth and home, Reader the thought of whom would trouble his waking hours and make sleep a dream, so that he dragged through the day, eyelids burning, and his feet like lead, *unable to make a fist*, your image having so undone him, and the sweet, nay, electric fantasy of taking you to some hotel where neither of you

1 – Or "sac," in the translation from the French *Fou de Coudre*, *The Forbidden Stitch* (A.L.G.W.U. publ.), where the original "reticule," rendered as "sac," in the 2009 Belgian edition, is found retranslated (Norton-Simon, *Let's Face Facts: The Uses of Perfidy*, op. cit.); cf. Bergson's disquisition, *On the Preference for the Tainted.*
2 – "Coffee," in the Peruvian edition.

---

* One more than Goldilocks.

were known, locking the door, and [erotica, T.K.], to recur; that phenomenon is the transposition, finally, of "magazine" into "museum" – where, in the eighteenth and nineteenth century, *magazine* was understood to mean a *depository* (as, a "powder" magazine), a *warehouse*, in short; and *museum*, a diversion, usually printed, upon which one mused (as, a periodic publication).

How did these two terms become transposed?

How would *I* know?

I construe my duty thusly: to draw your attention to the fact.

Now I am done. Now I may rest.

Now I may close my eyes, and, utilizing one of several techniques of oriental relaxation I have studied, pray for that momentary solace from, dear Reader, the vision, spectre, dream, or fevered fantasy, of [see above] . . .

O, Bongazine

Source: Annals of *Bongazine* (formally "*O, Bongazine*", *c.* 2031); from the song, by permission of the family of J. Pungeon and the Pungeon Estate, with special thanks to Muriel Pungeon-Kraft for the use of the captions.

I am privileged to quote *in its entirety* the note from Greind's (then) solicitor, Morris Schwartz, to Miss Pungeon (see below) and will take this opportunity to suggest that, *had the note been delivered*, the course of that enterprise* at the least and, most probably, of the organizations and endeavors allied to and dependent (at that time) upon it might have been altered for the better.

Dear Miss Pungeon –

I take the liberty to address these few lines to you, hoping that they, as has my suit, find favor in your eyes.

I thank you for taking time from your busy schedule, and I make bold to suggest I may perhaps begin to comprehend what that time means to you. For I, myself, am that which one might call "a busy man."

I find, in my own life, the adage, "if you want something done, give it to a busy man," apt. And I, once again, deign to suggest that I might expand or extend this self-observation to yourself.

I hope this gives no offense, as it is, first and last, my desire to *please.* (If the expression of thanks be not, at its core, no, let us rather say, if its *only allowable* purpose can be avowed as other than the discharge (be it happy or coerced) of debt.) (What point, then, in the pleasure of the debtor?)

Do I transgress the norm? So be it.

Pleasure, I say, where I have received so much, and that from the little word "yes." No lover, nay, no swain, mad fool, *et cetera*, inflamed by passion ever gained more happiness from that one syllable.

Nay, may we not observe that that man, driven by, at least in some measure, the desire to *conquer* found the enjoyment of his conquest, no, not "empty," but pale in contrast to his joy at the capitulation?

---

* *Bongazine.*

Not me.

Thank you thank you thank you. And, should Fate ever place me and I know myself to be in a position to return the favor, I can think of little which I would not do to do so.

Pray, do not construe these empty words.

Yours till the Gym Crows,

MORRIS SCHWARTZ, ESQ.

The sad, handwritten addendum, clipped to the page, "'Esq.' How tacky . . ." has been shown to be discontemporaneous with the "note of thanks." Many believe it to be a prank, or (harmless?) act of vandalism on the part of a (later) student, library employee, or perhaps (in a most intriguing suggestion) soldier at the time of the Museum's (first) occupation.[1]

1 – "Why the first occupation?" the attentive reader might enquire. Pray God I had the time to tell you.

The Death of My Kitten

Source: excerpted, with permission, from *O, Bongazine* (Canon of the Society, M.P.P.), 2039.

"Mieu, mieu, mieu," went the cat, as the car ran over her progeny.

She could not see it, being down below the windowsill, in her accustomed sunny quadrant of the new (peach) sitting room.

She could not see it* – but *Johnny* could.[1]

"The car," he thought, "didn't even slow down! It didn't even *slow down* . . ."

1 – "How wide his eyes grew, and how round – like drawings of eggs on a skillet, or like the old British penny . . ." Who *wrote* these words? Would anyone having the remotest clue please address him- or herself to the editors?

* The windowsill (?)

[Untitled]
From *Count Rumsford in Hell*, #2 in the series *Stories of Hearth and Home* (Scholastic Publications)[1]

"Oho," the Bimbashi said, and "Oho, Count Rumsford. How do we find you today?"

"I have a hangover," the reply came, "as big as King Kong's dick."

The wizened scribes nodded and smiled, each to himself, as he made those few marks which would, when transcribed, expurgated, and redacted, comprise first the official, and, upon the death of the principals, the sole record of the interchange.

"What the Sam Hill," the Count went on, "do we have to eat?"

"Yes," the Bimbashi said, and clapped his hands.

The curtains parted at the sound, revealing a huge pit, the pit filled with glowing coals.

At the pit's edge knelt a small elephant. At the elephant's side, a fellow with an axe.

The Count watched as this man began to tie a vast bandanna over the elephant's eyes.

This task completed, he then offered the creature a cigarette.

"We're having elephant," the Bimbashi said.

1 – A shelf corporation of *Bee-zine* – called into being at the time of "The Great Migration," and, originally a tax shelter for flight capital; *Bee-zine* has been identified as a financial *ruse-de-guerre* of Krautz. How telling, then, that it *made* money![A]

A – See also, *Two Trains Leaving Chicago*, op. cit.

A Disquisition on the Mud Pond

A Disquisition on the Mud Pond
or: *When Worlds Colloid*
Source: "Oh, Please", *Bongazine*, 2074,
© Goodstone Comix.

"How can we begin," he said, and it occurred to him as he said it, as it must have occurred to the more perceptive of his listeners – or, perhaps, say, not to the more perceptive, but to those *among* the more perceptive given to or appreciative of irony – that he had, of course, *already* begun, and employed this seemingly separate, modular, or Ciceronian construction as the beginning *per se* of an operation for which he was stymied to construe a beginning – not unlike the bath or shower shared by a couple whose relationship has progressed to the sexual, but who, having been separated for some time, now reunited, feel "shy."

"How can we begin," he said "to approach the, I will not say 'pond,' I will not say the 'pond,' no, but 'the phenomenon *of* the pond'? For to denominate the Mud Pond a 'pond' is as to attempt to plumb the meaning of a Christmas tree by a dissection of its needles. Nay, or of the holiday by a discussion of the tree."

Here he consulted his notes and died.

It has been remarked that his life, that *all* our lives (in, perhaps, an unwonted manipulation of the conceit) can be likened to the colloidal – to mulch, for example, or to "junket."

Now, discounting the, finally, one must say, precious appositeness of the simile applied to one whose life was *dedicated* not to the study of mud, but to the preservation, the, it will not be seen to be hyperbole to say, beatification (if one may use the term in speaking of a *place*) of the Mud Pond – discounting, as I say, and why should one not, for the pleasure of argument, which pleasure or inclination to same must be presumed in the readership, else why would they apply themselves to this otherwise arguably dry, scholastic tome?

(Or is there no one there? Is no one reading this, and am I going mad? How would I know if I were? Who would there be to tell me?

And whom could I believe? If I could not even credit the reports of my intellect, how could I those of the senses, whose dispatches must and can only be known as a distillate of the first-named organ?

Is it not fitting that I, who have worshipped it, should, like the so-trusted lieutenant or general of a dictator, should be the first to fall when that whim or psychosis previously turned against the external regime or enemy is practiced, as, inevitably, it must be, upon those who assisted in its overthrow, who know the dictator's weakness, his sadism, insecurity, instability, psychosis, screaming madness, in short – isn't that the way? Where did I go wrong?)[1]

1 – Here follows a list:

1 Should have been a fireman
2 Too much carbohydrates
3 Weak

And a fourth entry, scratched out and indecipherable. How may we interpret this "toying with madness"? Thank God such is not our job.

Get Dressed, You Married Gentlemen
or: *The Balaclava Helmet*, from *Tales of the Burn Bag* (*B-zine* Comix)

. . . when the nurses would emerge from the ambulance and heave the wounded on to the debris – that rousing sight – the white-coated practitioners streaking up, as their vans skidded, noses dipping and then their tires screaming their displeasure to the brake, as they gave up that part of their tread destined as an offering to fashion. What a scene! The burning of the wounded by the Ambulance Corps!

"I want to be," said the young James, "I want to be, I *will* be one of them, when I grow up."

And now, looking back on a career which spanned those four decades, he could hardly, even now, could hardly credit it had passed. It was done. He had done it. And it was time to remove the goggles, the frock, the bulbous-toed shoes, so oft the loving subject of the parodist – to remove them, and . . . to walk away? How could one walk away from it? The friends, the jokes, the stories, the membership in the World's Best Club?

He did not think of the prerogatives. He never had.

Not when this one or that had attempted to bribe him; not when, as daily happened, he saw envy in the eyes of a civilian – never. It was his job, his calling, and his duty, and that was the end of it. He glanced – could it be for the last time? – at the bronze plaque over the door – the figure of "Bootsie," and the words, now become so much a part of the culture, "Oh, what the hell . . ." with the ellipsis standing in for the true burden of the phrase, suspected generally, but known, in truth, only to the Service: ". . . I'm fucked, anyway."

Oh, the tradition, he thought. And the love of tradition. It had raised and clothed and led and conforted him through – he could not say his "working" life. It was his life. And what would remain now?

Years – any would be too long – of a retirement.

What sentence could he hear less welcome – and him a perpetrator of no crime except longevity?

Here the manuscript degenerates from doubtful into that which we must consider spurious. My reasons follow.

One. Change in typeface.

Two. Degeneration in orthography, e.g. "eksetera" (ms folio 17), where, previously both "etc." and "*et cetera*" are found. (This I must consider the most telling, nay, incontrovertible evidence of traduction of the manuscript. And any still supporting the notion of integrity I must consider obdurate, not to say partisan.

And to what end, I ask you, when the one author is dead, and any conceivable others unknown, conjectural; and, *had* they existed, remaining, of necessity, at this remove, unable to assert their identity(ies)?

In what, then, is this supposed scholarship? Must it not be, has it not, in fact, degenerated into a mere parlor game or *disons le mot* a neurotic self-proclamation, which latter is, today, my theme.

(Commotion on the floor. Sounds of a struggle in the ante-room, and the presence in the hall of the (masked?) (musked?) gunman, joined by several who had theretofore been unremarked, accepted as members of the Commission, these drawing from their sleeves or pockets black or navy-blue watchcaps, which, pulled over the head, proved to be balaclava helmets.)[1]

1 – The balaclava helmet was first used in the Crimean War (1857 *et ensuite*) as a facial protection from the cold, by British ranks:

Gimme my balacalava helmet, Lloyd, and pray
They stand down the firewood-gathering party.
I'm soon bound away in any case
Acrost that high-banked river
Known to us of old.
Ho, for a sojer's life.
Begorrah [etc.][A]

A – Flears' bubblegum cards of "Famous Occupations", series #5: Pipefitter, Crossing Guard, Dragoon.

The Halfway Point[1]

At which we are surprised to have our attention drawn to our progress; for, though it surely "bisects the material," it corresponds, rhythmically, to no inherited or learned predisposition for reflection or pause. It is an artificial period and, as such, it must compel our study. What was Krautz trying to say?

1 – This is not, as has always been apparent to anyone who takes the half-moment to consult the page numbers, the "halfway point" of *A Consideration* . . . – two choices offered us are:

(a) its designation is a joke, or error, or act of intellectual savagery;
(b) it is the halfway point of a shorter (or of another) work.

Dating the Material

Dating

This item was found in a shoebox in the Room, the dust jacket read, *Scilly, and the Channel Islands.*

It was not, of course, until the move to the New Museum that a careless workman (see below) dislodged the shoebox from its fixed position on the top shelf, and it fell, scattering the contents.

The museum staff rushed to restore the artifacts to their appointed and relative positions on the shelf (a task of no difficulty, as they'd been pictured, for long, on the schematic drawing at the entrance to the Hall). Schoolchildren of that age would have been able to recite by heart: "The card from the optician, half a sheet of stamps, illegible letter from what is believed to have been an office-seeker, throat sweets, guide to Scilly and the Channel Islands, *et cetera.*"

Can we imagine the surprise of those museum workers on discovering in this last, beneath its prosaic jacket and title, neath its dull, familiar cover, a tome of a somewhat different sort, entitled, *A Dating Strategy for the Ages*?

Now, I will not waste the reader's time with exegesis of the (to our modern eye) regressive, nay, it is, finally, not too strong to say "insupportable" notions[1] which this book contains – another age might find these "quaint." We cannot.

I will limit myself, and direct the reader's (kind) attention to another question altogether: *What happened to the travel guide?*

1 – The Victorians (1837–1901) spoke of the "five forbidden topics." They were: illness, wealth, religion, politics and servants. But their race is run. The Empire (sea power, funded through colonialism, slavery and opium) is reduced to some (limited) commerce in woollens and small, luxury leather goods. Time marches on. The working man was sloppy.*

---

* And he got what he deserved.

The Uses of Inaccuracy

Greind, and the Development of the Bungalow
or: *The Uses of Inaccuracy*[1]
Source: *Tales of the Fantasist*

In the bungalow, in the early twentieth-century longing for the bucolic, we see the first (architectural) expression of nostalgia/*Weltschmertz.*

Less than a hundred years into the Industrial Revolution, we see the mind of man grope backward toward the Farm.

While all sing tropes to the New, the Future, while in Paris the conjunction of the (if misunderstood) Japanese love of the floriform finds

1 – In the original, "Innacuracy." The debate has, no, I will not say "raged," but has continued and continues regarding the intention or lack thereof of the author.

Let me widen the debate.

Could this have been a jolly jest on the part of the compositor?

How we forget the lowly. How the wealthy and powerful (how the comfortable, in fact) overlook, nay, deny the sentience of their servants, gossiping in front of them as if they were deaf to all but the commands to fetch or carry.

Must it not have been ever thus!

Are those so treated (must they not feel themselves to be?) slaves, or slaves-of-a-sort? Is there not that in the employee–employer constellation militating toward abuse?

Of course there is. For if the employer is denied the *de jure* right of life-or-death, the power to deny livelihood keeps alive the more-than-echo of its terror.

Imagine the poor father of three* about to turn home.

After a long, worrying day at his desk or factory bench. The owner passes, and the employee does not, in the owner's mind, display sufficient deference.

Suppose the stopping bell has rung. The employee is no longer, then, "at work," but yet he stands upon the owner's ground, and the owner feels himself owed an acknowledgment. The poor employee, fatigued from his day, his mind turned to the concerns of home, perhaps has not even noticed his superior walking by – but let us not weight the dice with coincidence – let us say that he *has* noticed, but that, feeling it incumbent upon him to display acknowledgment (*after* the bell) masters both habit and inclination (why would he not be polite?) and exhibits, let us say, for the sake of argument, a bit of diffidence, say truculence, even.

In that brief half-second has not the employer *marked him down*, and will he not make haste to practice and to exercise the extent of that power he may display without discomfiture or censure upon the poor working man: demotion, dismissal, blacklisting – none beyond his power. And does he not explain his depredation to himself thusly: "Such behavior breeds anarchy and destruction of the public order?"

How this worker, should he never *suffer* any of the penalties suggested above, is

* Or four.

its expression in art nouveau, that paean to writhing sexuality so curiously cast (hidden?) in the realm of the dicotyledon, in the United States the bungalow proclaims the wish to return, no, not to the jungle, no, but to that state (in its ideal, imaginary, form) uniting the wild and (or, better) expressing the idea of the wild-subdued; or, better, the innate *harmony* in the wild, or, the "savage" as a misunderstanding of the innately sublime – where a basically Protestant world view perceives all strife as error, and Paradise not as a state-after-death, but the true nature of the world, could we but deal with the Irish.

This is the longing for the Farm, for that prelapsarian (imaginary)[2] state where cows would milk themselves, roosters crow only upon request, all days be those of late summer or fall, all boys wear denim and all girls gingham or calico, *and yet* exhibit at the merest invitation, sexual abandon[3] of a sort and degree unknown since the historic hubris of Mesopotamia.

---

still subject to anxiety over their very real possibility – the spectre of them, perhaps, sufficient to unman him[A] as he wrestles with the question: will the excellent man react when "the boss" walks by, and, if so, how is he, then, different from a slave?

Granted the degree of slavery, as of anything,[B] may vary, but *au fond* it is the same. Might not, *must* not, this downtrodden being seek both redress and solace in escape? In alcohol or drugs, or raucous sex, or sports, or good works, in neurosis; or in rebellion: in armed uprising, unionism, petulance, sabotage, absenteeism, goldbricking, sloppiness, and, perhaps, occasionally, the *jest*?

We relish, nay, cherish the employee's jest in its grandiose form: the cap of the Chrysler Building, the bi-cameral system, etc. – let us not forget it exists, also, in the day-to-day, offering an escape, a counterweight, a flywheel, if you will, for the otherwise potentially destructive anger occasioned by subservience. What force is worse than prejudice? What beasts, what "swine" we are – to class "the other" as a fit object for rage for (s)corn,[C] for dismissal – and how the example is given us, the response, not "in kind," not blow-for-blow, but in jest, in gentle cleansing jest, in humor, the (along with religion) solace of the weak.

I vote for it. I laud it. I praise those who practice it, and I *suggest* upon no evidence whatever, that the misspelling, "inaccuracy" [*sic*] *may* have been, *may* have been, I say, an intentional joke upon the part of the compositor.

A cheap theorem, you may respond. *No*, I reply, no, not a theorem at all – merely a suggestion.

2 – *Pace*, the Bible.

3 – See *The Hayloft*, vols IV–CXC.

A – Impotence, premature ejaculation, priapism, etc.

B – E.g. the temperature.

C – In the original "corn."

This is the bungalow, then.

The career of Greind at the Beaux Arts needs no elaboration here.[4] Suffice it to say [. . .][5]

4 – For a fuller discussion see *The Moving Picture Boys in Earthquake Land*, etc.

5 – Here the manuscript trails off into gibberish. The words at the bottom of page 12 alone standing clear: "Forgive, forget," and a telephone number, which legal restraints prohibit me from printing here, but which may be released to qualified individuals or institutions upon written application.

Lost

Lost

Source: "The Wars of the Lord," *Apocrypha*, vol. 3 no. 3

"Q. What if a book should be lost? What if a term should be lost – what would it mean if, without it,* it was reconstructed?† Would such increase our ignorance (for it would never be discovered)? And, on the other hand, what is our reason (thus, our history), save a procession of error?"

"Th'ain't nothin', and nobody there but us chickens."[1]

"Who *are* the Hittites, anyway? And what did we ever do to *them*?"

Oh, I don't know. "Lost,"[2] I suppose, although the very word seems to convey a foundation-of-meaning, an identity, if you will, far greater than any I enjoy. How odd is language, whereby, in identifying things, we "craft" them, we far-more-than-endow them, with the power to please, to terrify, to comfort. And how difficult to pierce its veil. To strike through to the *ding an sich* – to the meat of the whole dilemma, to which science a devotion is most usually accounted heresy – where Jack and Jim and Jones and Robinson say, "Do not affront me with your 'language,' your 'semantics,' your Jesuitical, Hebrew, Communistic, intellectual, fill-in-the-blank loathsome manipulation; but let me, I demand, dwell comfortable with my understanding of and application to the few works my betters have allowed me, and which talismans render comprehensible to me the world."

Times change. People change constantly, from conception till death

1 – In the original, *our* chickens. Jean Kerr, *The Ego and I.*

2 – Spectrographic analysis in 2121 (Bell Labs, Hot Coffee, Ar) revealed that the supposed "o" in "Lost" was, in fact in the original manuscript a "u", thus changing the meaning of the monograph considerably, and rendering its title, "And, Besides, the Wench is Dead," more comprehensible.[A]

A – Alternatively, "And besides, the witch is dead"[?], attrib. E. Y. Harburg.

* The term. † The book.

(exempting, always, middle age); and even after death they change (decay), leaving, for the moment, the (semantic) question of whether, at that stage, they are still "people."

Interests change, tastes change – the taste buds (on the tongue) grow ever less acute over time, and give rise to the sophistication (good? bad?) of the culinary arts.

But it has been said that the *past* does not change. What bullshit. How can we say that it does not change, if it is (*as* it is) unknowable?

Werner Heisenberg (1902–1978–1982) was one of the best-dressed men of his day. It was said that his penis was of a length and (when aroused) circumference to awake either anxiety or rapt attention in all who beheld it – but he is remembered, in our time, for quite another thing: his "uncertainty" principle. This held that it's impossible to know both the speed and the location of a sub-atomic particle (who would *want* to?); or, in layman's terms, where something is and how fast it's going – or, that the act of *observing* something alters the thing observed.[3]

Well, *sure*, and when's it more true, than of the past?

"O-ho," the phenomenologists say, "you can change the 'past'?" The answer is "Of course," that, like the householder, slave to the bank, to the boss, the media, controlled by a few blunt expressions – "country," "honor," "wealth," "the future," "democracy," "free," "on sale" – all are in thrall *not* to that power which can *manipulate* the physical world, but which *interprets* it.

3 – E.g. a little worm crawling on a leaf, the glance of an old, half-dead, stinking carriage horse in Central Park.[B] Consider: from Robert W. Service, *Tales of the Yukon and Allied Investigations* (Potlach Press, Hyder, Alaska, 1931), quoted by permission:

What do you think *now*, Jim McFay?
With your dogs all dead at the end of the day
With the wolves all a-singin' hush-a-bye
Would you sell your soul for a shot o' rye?
Would you trade your lungs for a gen-pox pipe?
Would you* [etc.][C]

B – Especially if one is not *in* Central Park at the time.

C – Generally understood as included as a "dog reference", cf. C. Suarez ("The Original Hairless Mexican"), *The Adumbration of the Canine.*

* Also rendered "Wood hue."

We have been raised and habituated to think of the past as "that which happened." In fact, it is no such thing.

The "past," reflection will reveal, is merely *our idea* of what happened. It has no connection *whatever* to the (should they, in fact, exist) actual events which have (perhaps) transpired. Even were we not manipulated by an outside (human) force, our memory is imperfect, our methods of recording liable to decay, loss and mistranscription (let alone analysis).

More to the point, our perception (that survival mechanism) is a frayed, self-referential device. It fits us not to perceive the world, but to survive it – i.e., to see, understand, and act upon the universe *only as threat* (i.e. that which must be subdued).

I will not even say all other information is discounted or ignored. No. I will say that anything not perceivable as threat is not accepted as information. It is not assessed, as it is not *seen. Et cetera.*

No. This notion that the "past" is something which took place is wrong.

It did not "take place." It is taking place now.

And the question is perhaps not why Greind (Bennigsen) wrote (as it seems likely that he did), "All is *lust*," but why it should interest us.[4]

4 – The response appears below:

Everything is sex.
Sex is sex.
Art is sex.
Literature is sex.
Marriage, death and government are sex.
War is sex.
Pictures of naked women writhing and pretending to have fun are sex.
Animals are sex.
Food is sex.
Other things are sex.
They're all sex.
(JACOB COHEN, *MARS*)

The Toll Hound

The Toll Hound

The Appeal to Caninity

I write of that collective history, that mass-race consciousness which does not name itself, but which is "culture"; where ten generations of schoolchildren have prattled that "There was a farmer had a dog, and Bingo was his name-o" – in the belief that "Bingo" was the name of the dog; whereas recent evidence has suggested most strongly, we may say incontrovertibly, that it was, in fact, the name of the farmer.

Earlier times delighted in the picture puzzle wherein a field of flowers held, on observation, a concealed numeral or face – those puzzles of figure-and-ground, where the viewer, once ignorant of the crypto-content, having once become aware of it, could never banish it from his or her mind.

Once the sign was a mere field, now it is a field in which there is a numeral.

Once it was a vase. The vase, however, was revealed to be the outline, the profile of two facing visages, *et cetera*, *et cetera*. (A testimony to an era much more easily amused – that time, we might say, whose *ur*-phenomenological bent was capable of being titillated by visual ambiguity.)

What can the modern philosopher make, however, of an ambiguity (say ambiguity or, if you will, "alternativeness")? For, though prima facie source work establishes the date of the song's first appearance, and the place – 1835, in Huguenot Louisiana, Priedieux Parish – the home, for eight generations previous, of the Bienguele – and though the clan was famed for, nay, though the name was synonymous with the breeding of dogs (some say with the actual creation of the Toll Hound), and though the phrase "adroit quant aux chiens comme les Biengueles" in the Cajun jargon[1] survived well into the twentieth

1 – Hi-John-the-Conqueron Morphée, "The man who wears the funny hat," *Legends of the Bayoux* (privately printed). Cf. Anon., *Muuguu: The Life of the Soul*, an informal survey of the folkways and the ceremonial food preparation of Priedieux Parish.

century, still, one might, from pique, or sloth, or intractability (for who can plumb the human mind?) stick at awarding a status greater than *probably* to the identity of the named figure.

How charming, again, that time, how dear; and how the contemplation of history brings us simultaneously, gently as the zephyr, to the twentieth, to the nineteenth, and, inevitably, to the eighteenth century – to that France, Mother of Irony, which awarded the name Bienguele – for what oddity, propensity or prodigality we can only surmise – to that expulsion from France, to the New World, there to pursue, we assume, the rituals (whatever they may've constituted) of the Protestant Rite.

I would beg the reader's indulgence to recur, for a moment, to the song itself.

Its first lines have already been quoted.

The burden, for those unacquainted, continues:

B.I.N.G.O.
B.I.N.G.O.
B.I.N.G.O.
And BINGO was his name-o.

How subtle, how lovely are the autonomic operations of a culture. Here, in a rhyme surviving for children, we find the reiteration, the insistence-from-the-grave, as it were, of the clan's claim that its reputation be acknowledged.

Driven from France, lost in the reductive combination and recombination which is Time. Still the name – separate from the entity, like a frog in a laboratory experiment whose limbs still respond, though sense is gone – lives on.

Still the name resonates, insisting on its right to be heard; on its right to fame as dog-fancier – it lives on. Its orthography simplified, yes, for the New World, but simplified (obscured) in the very service of survival, crying for redress, but blessed, in that the very generations of children, ignorant of the song's hero, their knowledge of the same only less than their apathy, that their prattle, though ignorant, was the vessel, and the only vessel, for this fragile memory, this voice from the grave.

It was not a dog. It was the *farmer* of whom the song spoke.

Found in a Trunk in Pinsk
Source: "Pepita, Chet and Donna," or "The Moving Picture Boys in Spain," from *The Cardiff Giant*[1]

To begin to understand the *Hundmotif* we must first acquaint ourselves, as in many other spheres, with the taxonomy of the breeder.

What are we talking about here? Setter, pointer,[2] hound, terrier, and, of course, spaniel.

Working breeds all, happiest when, under the direction of man, they turn their energies to the mutually beneficial task.

This task, be it shepherding, ratting, sport, chase, or what have you, blesses them both, as who that has witnessed can deny?

It is no apologia, that creed which holds that God appointed each his place, high and low, master and man, it is proved as a mere matter of observation; why, look at the bees, flitting now this way and now that, making honey for the delectation of the higher form, of man.

How unfitting, how terrible, how vile were the relationship inverted.

It is, of course, Greind's predilection for the canine which begets this endless scholarship – the (seemingly endless) outpouring of academic

1 – See also Jacob Cohen, *The Recurrence to the Canine in "Wilson"*.
2 – We are indebted past any rational hope of discharge to Fink, Poyle, et al., for their *Funny Bathroom Signs of Wisconsin.*[A] The index *alone* has had me chuckling many a long and otherwise tiresome suburban night.

A – The fame of which has been (in my opinion, undeservedly) eclipsed by Berg's *I Don't Swim in Your Toilet; Don't Piss in my Pool.* Cf. *"We Aim to Please; You Aim, Too, Please": The Legal Battles of Fink, Poyle* et al.

Can we account for critical taste? Can we account it "taste"? Must we not, rather, recognize it as the most pernicious admixture of vacancy and license?

Imagine a chap instructed, hired to form and express an opinion on a subject beyond his grasp. Imagine farther, this chap (self-selected, as we have seen, for his biddable cupidity), given the hint that his work will be better received should it be deleterious. Couple this with the natural antipathy of the emasculated for the well and active, and you've got a can of worms.

studies, which, were they to vanish, would force the library shelves to show their bare bottoms to the passing world.[3]

3 – Like a buncha whores.

The Sermon

Translated from the German. Re-issued, in the American adaptation, as "By Works or By Faith?" and, again, redacted and condensed and found as an interpolated aphorism in *The Toll Hound: Line Breeding in Louisiana, or Fifty Years of Coon Hunting* by "A Gentleman", in chapter 3, where it appears in the form, "What's Better, *Cake* or *Pie*?" It appears, again in an ecclesiastic setting, quoted in *I Know Where I'm Going*, a collection of sermons by J. Bienguele, St Antoine's Parish, Monkton, Louisiana, in the sermon, "Now Let's Talk About Dogs." This is the book found on the President's bedside table, the letter-opener holding his place, and his place *this very page.*[1]

How can a living God be both omnipotent and omniscient?[2]

1 – Cf. "The Shadowy Figure of Col. House", in *Edith Wilson and the Re-enactment of the Primal Scene.*

2 – Followed in a much more flowing, not to say "hurried" hand, these words: "Oh God, oh God, oh, I'm *so sorry*."

The Skunk[1]

Lots of things don't smell good,
but few do it on purpose, and
fewer still as their "best trick."
GINGER

". . . of the skunk, as it wandered
across the road with the well-
known peculiar gait, which,"
et cetera.
"THE OLD WRANGLER RIDES OUT"

Which garnered this – we leave to the reader to determine if deserved or not – critique:

That anyone acquainted with the animal well knew the gait with which it wandered and that others learned of it only from the author's promiscuous and false (to *them*) assurance of its currency. That, then, the description of the gait were supererogatory, or a Ciceronian device – a, if not *fiendish*, at least false attempt to win the friendship of the audience by ascribing to it an unwarranted conversation with the Wild.

Many, at the time, found his absorption with the issue picayune; and the proverbial "correspondence which would fill volumes" *did*, in fact, expand and occupy and was presented in two volumes[2] and consisted of letters to *The Times*, the responses of its editors and readership responses to *these*, and the subsequent general outcry. Which is memorialized and survives in the pictographs of graffiti, skywriting, and monumental art.[3]

Someone once wrote, "O, Death, Where is thy Sting?"

1 – Its inclusion in this section generally accounted a *jeu d'esprit*, or "brainfart" on the part of the Fantasist, for the skunk, *Mephitis mephitis* (Lat.), is related *if at all*, not to the *dog*, but to the *weasel*. 'Nuff said.

2 – E. K. Byrnes, *Toujours Perdrix?!* and *The Charles River Whitefish* (Sunset Press).

3 – "This correspondence now must cease," as displayed in *Cute*, the Journal of the Architectural Society, © Elders of the Architectural Society. Cf. ibid., "Carved in Stone, Written in Blood: The Curse of the Bambino."

The answer, to those unfortunates in the editorial offices of *The Times*, proved to be: 16 Regent Street, Fourth Floor, on which we may assume they meditated for the space of five floors[4] at the rate of 32 feet per second per second.

"One riot, one Ranger," wrote the anonymous Texan.

And well might the cleaning staff so tragically mistaken for the editorial have lamented the absence of that one Ranger that cold fall day which proved to be their last.

And would it, as has been argued elsewhere and at length, have been more or less of a tragedy had the staff actually been engaged in those activities to which the mob took exception?

At what point (put differently) does the tragic become the pathetic, and vice versa?

Is the discussion of the above a tacit approval of the possibility of, at some point, an exculpability on the part of the rioters?

Theoretical ethics being beyond the scope of this investigation, we leave the readers to their own determination, and return to the *primum mobile* of the unfortunate affair.

The question, which the furor raised from the category of aesthetic to ethic, might, had the times been more leisurely or the populace that way responded, have been elevated to the level of metaphysics. (Though another might invert or rearrange the offhand (for which I beg the reader's indulgence) hierarchy in which I have ordered them.)

Right reason might say that those conversant with the gait of the skunk – that odd, disjunctive half-lope which, at speed, invites the viewer to consider it a progress "sidewise," the hindquarters disposed not in line, but some 10 to perhaps 20 degrees out of the line of progress – required no gloss upon it, while those non-conversant might be better served by a straightforward note.

And that the latter would, if executed frankly, have partaken less of the character of a digression than did the, we must say, coy attempt to sneak in the description as part of the burden of the piece.

4 – The floors being numbered, of course, in the European fashion – that counting the first, in their system, being the second in ours, and that which we know to be the first having no particular worth at all in their determination. I recommend to the reader D. S. Winicot, *Where Is the First Floor?* (D.I.Y., 19??).

A stylistic solecism?

Making an end, one must, I feel, say "yes"; a fatal disqualificative flaw, however? Under what possible Draconian, nay, psychotic, nay, incomprehensible system of values?

Thus arising the question, and, thus, the popular unrest occasioned by the minor, momentary, pardonable (if other than worthy) jejunity, and its major, extensive, tragic incomprehensible outcome.

Other Breeds

Found in a bottle off the coast of Spain, 2123.

At the Fish Orgy the Carp Was All Over the Plaice

. . . devoid of manners, like the rich, that subhuman spawn, forever pushing in line or making war, or sophisticating the good brew of those stout fellows, those princes of Christendom, the poor, or working poor, or lower middle class, or great unwashed.

But at the fish orgy
The slithery-slimy half-deniable glance or wink
Of the nictitating membrane – oh-so-saline –
Tolled the tail.

The rich ate fish eggs.

The "great unwashed," in this instance, could be said to be the crew of the *Mandragora*, inbound to Tenerife with a load of jute. This coaster was renowned for her part in breaking the blockade in the '94–'99 unpleasantness – in her mad dash to Newcastle with a cargo of coal.

Contemporary photographs show her funnel holed in several places, notably dead center of her corporate chop, the "terrier."[1]

Much has been written on the adoption by a Spanish company of the, finally, Celtic breed, in preference to the notably* Iberian "spaniel."

We will here occupy ourselves with two points of the argument: (1) whose business is it, anyway? and (2) perhaps they just "thought it was a good idea."

1 – i.e. center-of-mass – "a killing shot." *Not*, as has been otherwise bruited, struck in the "epicenter," which point could, of course, be determined only through abstruse applications of the calculus interesting to no one this author is capable of imagining.

---

* In fact, eponymously.

(1) Whose Business Is It, Anyway?

This says a lot.

For how much of our lives, if we think about it, comes down to just gossip? Most? All? Surely more than "some."

That being the case, wouldn't it do to, once in a while, just "give it a rest"?; because, if we think about it, what difference does it make?

It is just something that we do to feel important.

(2) Perhaps They "Just Thought It Was a Good Idea"

All of us have had this same experience.

It is part and, one might say, it is the *identifying* part of being human – the capacity for ideation – the ability to "think," to "project," to "imagine," to do this or that for "no good reason at all," if the spirit moves us.

For is it not, finally, the "spirit," the "indefinable," which gives to any art, to life, in fact, that "extra something"?

I think so.

And so the boat sailed on, its hold full of treacle.

And the sun, rising, as per usual, in the East, glinted on the (clear?) glass of the bottle, and the note* was found.[2]

2 – Substantial scholarship suggests the hypothesis that the dog was a (badly drawn or imagined) spaniel. This, I feel, begs the question in a particularly dumb way. For did not and does not the same power or office, spirit of being or force dictate and control both choice and ability? I am sure it does.

* Poem?

The Dunes

From "The American Traveler Series", pamphlet #4:
Motorcade – A "Picnic-on-the-Go"

We have been told "Abraham Lincoln" wrote the Gettysburg Address on the back of an elephant.*

Why have we been so informed?

Cui bono, as the Latins said.

Implicit, also, in the phrase, is the postulate, "'Abraham Lincoln' wrote the Gettysburg Address."

We do not *know* who wrote it.

"Who would profit?" we must ask, from acceptance of the asseveration?

All the principals are dead, and there is nobody here but you and me.

More accurately, of course, there was nobody there but *him*. What is this schizoid bifurcation of the self into "Thee and Me," speaker-and-listener (lion and tiger [*disputed*])?

Is it the piprucuct† of that cruet‡ though accidental incarceration, or was that boo boo just the happy hook upon which propensity for chat was hung?

What can it mean, this "you and me"? There was nobody there but *him*, and, it must have seemed to any but the most deluded mind,§ no possibility of any eventual discovery. For the Craft, the Capsule (was it not), having missed "rendezvous," was inexorably bound beyond the Moons of Jupiter, bound into that which prior time, in charming ignorance, denominated "illimitless space."[1]

But, "How Mighty is Allah to Save!" – so wrote the ancient desert folk.

1 – Or "limitless space," the two being, generally, held identical. Cf. Flammable and inflammable. For a discussion of which, please see *The Consulting Fireman*, which survives, in part, in holograph, for those of that bent.

* "Envelope?" Disputed. † "Biproduct?" ‡ "Cruel?" § A-ha.

And where is it found truer than in this extraordinary case? Nowhere.

The Toll Hound

[Here follows an interpolation of *The Meeting on the Strand*. Rabbi Zadok Ben Ezra (Zabazz) writes[2] that the placement is mere accident, and that "accidents happen" – a phrase which has entered the language.]

The Meeting on the Strand

"Woof. Woof. Woof." Pause.

"Come along, Buddy," said the boy. "Ain't nothing but a squir'l, or chipmunk. 'N they're more scarit of you then you are of them."

But the boy looked around, and realized there was no chipmunk, for the beach was wide, and they had wandered to the verge.

The tide, receding, had left a good two hundred yards of smooth, hard-packed sand between them and the dunes. The moonlight showed that there was nothing between the two save him and his dog. He looked around and saw that, now, in fact, there was nothing but *him*. He saw the pawprints receding, back over the beach, and heard the last frightened vocalizations of the dog's flight, and then he was alone, stopped by some force, some unassailable energy of anticipation – some deep-seated sense of . . .

Then the moonlight showed red; the moonlight seemed, he would therever after remember it, as the source (imagined? physiologic?) of the carminization.*

Was it his mind's blood, obscuring his vision? Or, or could it have been Mars?

Yes, he thought. Mars – coloring the very moonlight, asserting its sway, stating the theme, if you will, of all that was to follow.

Yes, the moonlight turned red, in that instant, and, at once, he saw, in his periphery, that which, now save the waves, was the only motion in the still, still night.

2 – *Three Cohens in the Fountain.*

---

* Of what "turned it red."

Upon the cliff, the *Toll Hound*. Dancing, leaping in the moonlight.

To lure what? he thought. To attract what? For, certainly, the dog focused its efforts, as it was bred to do, upon the sea.

As it was bred to do, yes, but there were no birds upon the sea, no birds there to lure. And never had the dog danced at night.

Why, then, did it dance, and for what quarry? Jacob Cohen thought.

His eyes turned seaward, less for information than for relief, as if it offered a blank vista upon consideration of which he could form his thoughts. And, so, he rested his eyes upon that which, he supposed, would offer the least distraction. What historic miscalculation. For, there, bobbing in the waves he saw, he was the first to see, the Capsule.

Capsule Note

Did it all "come together in the Capsule"?

Did it all "come together on the Shelf"? *May* we allow ourselves the *purely* suppository hypothesis? The inversion, again, *purely* as a jest, or exercise, that the Shelf was not found in the Capsule, but vice versa – that the Capsule was discovered "on the Shelf."[1]

1 – See also *Moses and the Tablets, or Take Two and Call Me in the Morning.*[A]

A – I believe this marks the first uncensored appearance of "the Capsule Note" and I must ask: "What was all the fuss about?"

Bootsie and the Bootsie Clubs

Bootsie and the Bootsie Clubs
From *Whippies*

The whippers-in had lost their respect for the Master.

How could one tell?

One could tell from that, to the uninitiated, infinitesimal hesitation before their response to the horn. (To the Members of the Craft the gap was lengthy beyond measure.) How long ago that morning seemed.

"D'ye ken John Peel?" they all had joyous sung, pledging their allegiance in that dawn "doch an dorris" of mulled wine – that frosty dawn, with all eyes turning to the Portal, whence would issue George Wilson Brentum MFH, the God of the Bennington Hunt. Renowned for his dramatic gestures, "Bootsie's" invariable use was to appear at the close of the first verse, magnificent in his worn pinks, and cast his eye over the field, his myrmidons, from the right, then sweeping left over the huntsmen, whippers-in, boys, riders, grooms, well-wishers, over the whole of the County, come for the parade, for that panoply which was to each, in his way, England . . .

And how they sang! Each with a voice which "had no bottom," on their "view" of his beloved, craggy face.

For who among them did not have his tale – of Bootsie's humor, of his knowledge of the woods, of the fox, of weather, of that most prized and useful of understanding, Human Nature?

["How Bootsie Lost His Voice"][1]

1 – Omitted from the original. Discovered in a "saratoga" trunk in Alexandria, New Egypt, in 2191, the later-interpolated "How Bootsie Lost His Voice" will, of course, be found at this point in the narrative in the majority of subsequent editions. It was, of course, adjudged spurious by the 22nd Lateran Council,[A] but, as it has found its ineradicable place in our hearts, it will be found below.[B]

A – See *Bullshit*, Proceedings of the Council, 2193.

B – Cf. *How Bootsie Lost His Whip*, vol. 2: *The Variants* (Philovolpian Society, 2199),

And here the voices slowed, stilled, and stopped.

This one or that, involved with one last adjustment, one last needless tug on the stirrup or martingale, remarking the abrupt termination of the song, looked up, followed the eyes of the crowd to Bootsie, standing in the Portal; and, seeking the cause of what could only be understood as the crowd's shock, found, at his feet, not the accustomed beagle, "Sally", not a beagle at all – but a Toll Hound.

The silence of the crowd was deep and wide and endless – not to be measured in time, but out of Time, as it were – as, for them, Time had stopped, and would not be set right again until they had received an explanation.

And thus they stood. Until Bootsie, drawing himself up, let fall his hand upon the dog's collar and spoke. "I don't care," he said. "I love him."

How Bootsie Lost His Voice

"No, I am vile. And I am sick. I am a fornicator," he thought. He stared at his bleary eyes in the cheval-glass, and he shook his head. Overcome by weakness brought on by this acute self-assessment, this self-loathing, he sank down on to the padded bench. His head hung down. His breathing became shallow, and his thoughts (if they could be called "thoughts," for they were feelings, rather, an emission of that deepest part of the soul – of that pre-verbal knowledge which is the wisdom of the proto-being, of Adam before the Fall – which is, perhaps, knowledge of God.

The knock came at the door and he hopped toward it, his tail fluffy and erect, his ears twitching.

---

which treats of the (inevitable) congruent, "How B. Lost His: Boots, Shoes, Cane, Cape, Life, Voice,[B1] Good Name,[B2] etc."

B1 – The inclusion of "Bootsie/Voice" has been definitively linked to the much earlier "tales" of Kate Willingsley, as part of the "Bootsie" stories, that series of successful children's books whose hero was a pink rabbit with white feet ("Boots").

It has been sugested that this "Alexandrian Link" may be inverted. That we may, in fact, as with Klein's bottle, "jump in at any point" and name it the beginning (opening). Or, to be round, suggest that Kate Willingsley (in reality Arthur Wingsleye Brown, 1906–1959) created his pink rabbit in homage to that Master of Fox Hounds. But who cares?

B2 – Never substantiated.

For he knew that this was Flora, with his plate of sprouts and leaves.

The door swung open.

"Oh, *Bootsie*," she said. "Oh, my best wee darling. Is it *hungry*? Is it only the most famished little *thing*? Look what I've brought you!"

She set the plate down upon the floor. And, as she did so, he spied on it his favorite treat: carrot tops! She had remembered!

The Club

For nothing can grow, save it grows in something.
KRAUTZ

I write of the Club, for it has been insufficiently written of. What were the Crusades, but the[1] Field Days of a Club?

What the great days of the Universities, their appurtenances, the cracked leather armchair and the meerschaum pipe supplanting the halberd, mace and sword of the preceding example?

And the Masons of old, who designed the Pyramids, the cathedrals, and so on – that confraternity, known to "meet Wednesday" at that local eatery, and whose endorsement of the same betrayed generations of wayfarers into a gastronomic Bad Half-Hour – what were they but a Club?

It is, I believe, not only a natural but an inevitable expression of the human need for companionship.

No hermit forms a club. No. For, even could they overcome that antipathy which would seem to be the *sine qua non* of their profession, what would they discuss?

No. For we see the essence of the Club is that most pleasant fiction: that its members have something in common.

A strict analysis would, I am afraid, in most cases reveal that this common treasure (for treasure we must count it if it Grease the Ways of Fellowship) is, in most or many cases but a subscription to that pleasant fiction.

But what's wrong with that?

Yes. It is a "device" – like marriage, education, like, for that matter, a toaster.

Do they not all stem from the great consciousness, "the All,"* and to That Great End the identity of which eludes us?

The Club, I say, that socio-anthropologic "campfire" – that meeting place, that better-than-home – for rather than the paradigm "a barn-

1 – Attenuated, granted.

* Maybe.

yard in the rain," or, better, of that sack containing monkey, chicken, snake and goat into which the convicted felon was sewn, which was than tossed into the Tiber – rather than the template or example, I say, of these, which we can recognize as the Type of the Nuclear Family, the Club typifies the "Waterhole," where, we are told, the feuding beasts set quotidian, usual, nay, inherited antipathies aside, and drank.

All* are different, and all are alike. They share (as above) a subscription to the ethos of the small, self-constituted tribe, and they share an objective: to make the members "feel good."

This goal, disguised, as in the more Puritan, confused or academic times it must be, is none the less found universally, and, should study not discover it, the object under observation cannot be a club.[2]

The Bootsie Club existed to impart to its members a feeling of connection to the past, in studying the arcana, in trading artefacts, and in the search for relics, its members engaged in that benign and fond ancestor worship which, in its non-aligned, spontaneously occurring, individual expression, was known as "antiquing."

Let us examine the word. It is the present participle, or "gerund."[3]

The nominal form is "antique," meaning "an object of antiquity."[4] Thus, the noun–verb form (*qua* verb)[5] must mean "to look for antiques." Considered as a straight-up present participle, however, its true meaning is revealed, for here we see emerge the sense "to make (or 'to cause to appear') antique"; i.e. to form into a simulacrum of the antique, to add provenance (or its appearance) to.

We must, I feel, concede that this is the objective of many a member of a club.

It certainly was the goal of Jacob Cohen, that spring day on Mars.

The Bootsie Clubs offered to the youth of that day a sense that they were engaging in what used to be called "history," and that, in so doing, they were fulfilling the wishes of their ancestors. This was the great attraction of the clubs.

2 – It may be, to pick the two most likely examples, a religion or a committee.
3 – See issue #4.
4 – An "old thing."
5 – Gerund. See issue #4.

---

* Clubs.

And it is this sense, this sense of calm, of purpose, of "connectedness," which pervades Cohen's writings. His ostensible subjects – The Old Wrangler, Pre-Martian Dendrochronology, The Fantasist, The Mall, etc. – are, of course, of worth and weight and importance to dispute which would, rightly, brand one as a blatant and jejune fool. And those looking for an endorsement of that unfortunate position will have to look elsewhere.

But, I say, or, perhaps better, "and," those writings have a secondary, or, perhaps, additional, or, better, *alternative* excellence: they each can be understood as a treatise on Club Life.

Here, for example, is Cohen, in his Commencement Address to the Martian Dragons (the "doch an dorris"):

. . . that farewell, that setting-off ceremony, which, as we "turn the tapestry," we see speaks not of Adventure, but of its opposite. Not of peregrinations, but of Domesticity."

Here, I believe, the point is made.[6]

6 – Others, of course, "begged to disagree." Notably, the editor(s) of *Bongazine*, in their "GO BACK TO MARS!!!" (redacted and condensed in the more widely known (pamphlet) form, *Keep Your Pagan Feet off the Mall!* (Mud Pong[A] Press)), and Bennigsen, in his *Jane of Trent: A Life.*

A – In the original, "Pond."

Gentlemen

Generally identified as the "Married Gentlemen" of Section One (see page 111).

Now, it is said the code of the Gentleman is never to tell a lie. The code, of course, did not extend to his dealings with the shopgirl he seduced, the tradesman he defrauded, the workers in his family's enterprise he worked to death – but, to the members of his immediate class and caste, his small "tribe," in effect, the fiction held he told the truth. He was free to represent to himself that he told the truth to all people as those to whom he lied, those outside his caste, were not, by his definition, "people."

Memoirs[1] of a Man Who Ate Somebody[2]

1 – It has been established that this (*Memoirs*) is in fact the source of the (so famous) quotation. Its location needs no gloss here, neither the material into which it is carved, nor the style of the carving, no.

That which I today present to you is an expatiation, rather, upon that which gave rise *to* the quotation's fame. And I do not mean its reason or wisdom, no, nor to the fame of the book from which it comes, nor to the excellence of its redaction, no. Rather I direct your most kind and appreciated attention to that *instrument* which is responsible for its persistence through the years – that instrument which I believe must be the first tool of data storage: to the *chisel*[A] and to the derivative, vulgar, axiomatic "chiseler," and "better than a poke in the eye with a sharp stick."

Let us consider the latter first – the so-well-known construction which began small, and accreted (not unlike the coral, that remarkable creature which built the atolls) thusly:

1 Better than a poke in the eye
2 Better than a poke in the eye with a stick
3 Better than a poke in the eye with a *sharp* stick

I leave, for the moment, the moot point: which is better, a poke in the eye with a stick, or a poke in the eye with a *sharp* stick[B] and conflate, for that which I sincerely hope will be your diversion, the more overtly sexual condignity:

A – And to its drotomdical form, "the shard stick."

B – Better for *what*? For the purposes of this, finally, meaningless *bon mot*? For the *eye*? For *what*?

I wouldn't kick her out of bed on a cold night to hear her go thump on the floor.[C]

Let us follow the logic of the case:

1 I wouldn't kick her out of bed
2 On a cold night
3 To hear her go thump (on the floor)

We must, I think, accept the third phrase *toute entière*, as tempting as it may be to bifurcate the thing; for, finally, the appositeness of "to hear her go thump" can only be assured/assumed/accepted by a pre-facto understanding that "on the floor" is (as it must be) implied.[D]

And, further, we must say that the third and final module is not "supererogatory," which is, after all, the point of the whole ironic exercise, but *vitiating*, as it points out on the part of the writer *two conflicting motives*:

1 To keep warm
2 Percussion

The two, in conjunction, violating the (observed? implied? indwelling?) rule of irony: the simply oxymoronic or hyperbolic opposition, where (a), in being denied, is, in fact, affirmed.

By the light and direction of which rule we must see the strength of the construction weakened.[E]

2 – Cf. *Maritime Anthropophagy, or That's Why They Call Him Captain Cook*, publication of the HMS *Aurora* Society, Jubilee Issue: "We're Here, and We're Staying" (1987).

C – *Is* it more sexual?

D – The *thump* otherwise, attributable to the kick, or to a verbal or preverbal idiosyncrasy on the part of the victim.

E – Consider: "better than a poke in the eye with a sharp stick previously used to stir soup."

Bootsiana

Source: Dornford Yates, *The Muff Diver*

Is there life after birth[1] [*sic*]
Or is it just, not to
put too fine a point on it,
"a lot of nothing"?

1 – We would assume the author here intended *death*, and that we had been granted a rather delightful example of the "Freudian slip," were it not that the original (manuscript) title of the poem was "Placenta."[A]

A – Also the name of the author's country house in Berks.* [A1]

A1 – "What is the connection between *Berks* and *Placenta*?" asks the twenty-first century commentator (*The Narrow Way: Responsa Literature of the Shires*, Leeds: Halachic Press, 2111).

See also *Memories of the Berkshire Hunt*, by "A Member." Long attributed to G. W. B., or "Bootsie," this is the slim volume which is "The Book in the Case" at Roycroft, the site of the (second) original Bootsie Archive. As scholarship has disproved any connection between the book and either the aims, the members, or the history of the Bootsie Clubs, its display suggests either a love of whimsy congealed into tradition, or an obduracy bordering on the deranged.

* Berkshire, England.

The First Mention of "The Capsule" [1]

1 – This is generally accounted the *seventh* mention of the Capsule. The numerologists of the time of "The Great Decampment" suggested that the primes 1 and 7 suggested the absence of the immediary primes 3 and 5.[A]

A – Which, it has been further suggested,* equals 8, which is not a prime at all, and, so, what are we talking about?

* Established.

Weebut

"Could Weebut Recall That Sweet Moment Sublime"
See *supra.*

But who *was* "Weebut," when all was said and done; and, as importantly,* *was* all said and done? (For, must not a man make an end?)†

Yes, we have "'Robin Hood' of the Old West," and, on the other hand, Don ——, "who dared attack my Chesterton."

Whom do you like in a fair fight?

In the words of Lady Astor, "Always bet on the one with the biggest butt."

In which case, there you are.

A recurrence to the steatopygian, or is it just one of those cases where one hears a word for the first time in the morning, and, before bedtime, has heard it several times more? (Well, this is a fine way to "wish away" history, and, in fine, all knowledge – but why would one wish to?)[1]

1 – Pique, boredom, rage, an inexplicable propensity to mischief . . . The list is endless.[A]

A – The list, of course, is not endless, but, rather, screamingly finite, being limited to but four terms.

The author, we believe, means to suggest that the list *could* be infinitely expanded. But even here he errs, and, perhaps, more egregiously; for in his primary assertion he makes a (granted, rather stunning) error of fact – a mathematical solecism, whilst the implications implicit in his second assertion suggest egoism, nay, suggest self-idolatry and, thus, a spiritual malaise so deep and necessarily destructive as to make an error in arithmetic positively charming in comparison: it is the difference between "Give me a lever and a place to stand" and "Give me a lever or I'll blow your head off". See Mott's

The difference is vast
The difference is unbridgeable –
She is so far above me.
Oops! She's coming down now –
Here she comes . . .!
(Quoted in Masterman, Polley and Winocur, *Our Feral Young.*)[A1]

A1 – Found on the Shelf in the Capsule, in position 3. This volume was long considered a page-

* *More* importantly, *more* importantly. † Ha ha.

holder.* This is, I believe, the first supportable application of its contents.[1A]

1A – Though much has, of course, been made, numerologically, of its *position*, cf. "Goldilocks and the Three Bears", etc.

* Between volumes 2 and 4.

His Epitaph
Found in a trunk in Herts*

He was a true psychotic, and an artist only by courtesy.

The epitaph is widely (universally) known. But how its meaning has been traduced by its truncation! Let us, in the always informative, if, sometimes, painful, process, examine the original:

He was a true psychotic, and an artist only by courtesy – has anybody seen his *watercolors*???[1]

1 – Actually, *gouache*. (The difference between the two,[A] and its importance in this instance, having been exhausted in "Just Keep It Out of the Rain" (editors of *Vogue*), I will not touch upon it here. Suffice it to say that a too early exposure to the Lake Poets most surely and egregiously warped Greind's aesthetic sense, and that this writer concurs with Reb Bartholomew in the opinion that "any of his [Greind's] endeavors:

A – The difference between watercolor and gouache is one of *opacity* – the latter generally being held to've been executed using a large concentration of gum arabic, or other fixative, thus rendering the medium (and, thus, the result)† closer, in resemblance, to *oil painting* than to *watercolor*.

Semantically, the terms and their use are differentiated even (and, perhaps, especially) in the absence of this information, by the supposition (on the part of the speaker) that *use of the latter* (gouache) bespeaks a greater acquaintance with the question, and can, thus, be (even in ignorance), applied equally to an (optional) subgenre of Fine Arts containing both and perhaps all species of admixture of design media in which the pigment is diluted (and fixed) with water.

This acceptance of (and, perhaps, truth to tell, preference for) inexactitude in dealing with those occupations not considered suitable for the gentry dates, of course, to the Victorian (AD 1836–1901) freak that the nobility should not know how to do "one goddamned thing."[A1]

Interesting aberration.

What a funny time. What did they fancy? Stiff collars, whipping (as a diversion), horses and dogs. Funny old time.

And how will they look back on us, our progeny, I wonder, "in our fog"?

If we knew, should we alter our (to them, certainly) pathetic folly?

It is too late. It is much too late.

A1 – Except deal with (a) horses and (b) *dogs* [emphasis in the original].

---

* Hertfordshire, England. † Not necessarily.

painting, drawing, verse, drama, or song remotely classifiable as 'art' rather than otherwise 'smelt of wet dog.'")[B]

QUESTION: Does the degree to which the symbolic partakes of the absolute vitiate its (symbolic) power?

We must note that Goebbels said, "When I hear the word 'culture,' I reach for my Browning Automatic." Did ya think he could eradicate the Arts with a 7–13 shot *handgun*?[C]

His untimely demise ensures that we will never know. But, to return to the wider questions: How does a wet dog smell? And: Why should we find that offensive?

Obviously, the more "doggy" will not: the British, Anglophiles, sheep-herders, lesbians, and many of the overtly sentimental among us may find the scent – and, indeed, anything pertaining to the canine – somewhere on the scale from inoffensive to pleasant to provocative (and, perhaps, to extend the scale, to irresistible, and, perhaps, intoxicating, *et cetera*, *et cetera*).[D]

Well, hell, it's just an *animal*, and what do we think *we* (humans)[E] are, anyway?

Animals – one and all. Vicious, self-delusive beasts. Bad models, and bad company. So *what* if he read the Lake Poets? Must we then say that it's "catching"?

What is our concern with *germs*?

Is* homosexuality, AIDS, flu, cancer, artistic sensibility "catchy"?

If not, why, then, this constant preoccupation with the "smell of dogs" – I just don't get it . . .

B – As they were found in a trunk in the eaves of the tackroom, "The Copse", Bromley, Herts, it's not surprising.

It has been suggested that Bartholomew means his indictment to be taken not as sarcasm, but as reportage. *But could it not be both?*

C – It is, perhaps, not inapposite at this point to refer to the riddle of Goebbels, and his brown hen, "automatic." ("Whenever I hear the word 'culture,' I reach for my brown hen, 'automatic.'")[C2]

D – In the third edition, "*et cetera.*"

E – Episcopalians? See Chuck Scott, *That Darn Terrier*, chapter 4.

C2 – Evalyn Trudgely-Worth, *She Lays Eggs for Gentlemen: George Goebbels and the Riddle of the Bootsie Clubs*, and the inevitable *She Lays Down for Gentlemen: The Life of Evalyn Trudgely-Worth* by "A Colleague."†

* Was. † "A Collie"???!!!

Flight from Egypt
From: *Wars of th' Lord*[1]

"The parameters," he said, "the parameters, if I may, and who would refuse me?" Here he fairly glared. His glance taking in the entire room, not one of the occupants of which would have opposed his slightest wish, let alone an asseveration so obviously of the premier importance to him.

"The parameters," he said, "of Ritual Murder."

Here he tugged at his lapel, and cleared his throat, the two gestures having become so associated in the mind of his congregation that many, upon reflection, might have perceived that they understood their relationship to be one of cause and effect; and those better acquainted with the psychologic processes might well have reflected that, after a lifetime, the once accidental, then habitual, juxtaposition may have – indeed must have – become inevitable (and those further interested and versed in the intricacies of the physically pathologic may have wondered, given the symptom, if its subsequent exhibition may not have, in fine, brought about the somatic reality). (But must not each have regarded, and, so, understood the gesture from his own individual bias and perspective? The tailor, for example, musing on the torque transmitted to the cloth, the facing, binding, interfacing, etc., of the constituent layers of the lapels; the presser, if such there were in the room, on the havoc played with their, one would have to allow, most elegant roll, etc.)

"For the Book," he said, "is nothing less – though it is, of course, much more – than the catalogue *in esse*, and the opposition to, *in posse*, that ritual murder, that obeisance finally, that fratricide to which I devote our brief hour together this fine Sabbath morning. For I ask you to consider the tale of the Flight from Egypt. Let us take the elements:

1 – The "Trent" Saga: *Trent's Lost Case*, in Anton de Meulemestière ("Scruffy"), Belgian National Archives, Neue Zeebrugge, Mars.

the children thrown into the river, the Angel of Death descending upon the Egyptian firstborn, the flight of the Jews, their passage through the sea, and their subsequent situation, alone and afraid, in the wilderness.

"Now let us, as it were, write these 'headlines,' or 'headings,' each upon a card, and toss them in a hat."

Each member of the congregation visualized, as he spoke, his own hat. And, as the words left him, he realized that they did, and that such might, nay, could, nay, with the blessing would offer a most promising topic for a future sermon.

He saw or rather felt the sermon take form, whole, in his mind's eye – this one understanding "hat" to mean the daily trilby, bowler, Homburg; that woman, the veiled feathered *confectionnerie* of fashion, the children free to understand it as the mood and perceptive capacity fitted it: a sailor hat, perhaps, a motorman's hat, the soldier's helmet; and the practitioners, of course, of these professions, understanding it as use had habituated them – each hearing the term as who could say "random" history – if such there were – had fitted him. And if such were true, as each of them knew it true, of a simple hat, how much more true of the Name of God?

The faint, not inattentive, and not yet impatient, but inquisitive, polite, one might say, responsive murmur, or, better, rustle of the congregation brought him back to his text.

"– in a hat," he said.

"And then, were we to pick them out, and spread them on a table, might we not understand their possible reordering *thus*:

"That they sacrificed children, that they fled from, or *abandoned* the practice of Infant Sacrifice; that, is passing through the sea they were, we might say, "reborn," *but* reborn, reborn or reconstituted *with this difference*: that they, having abjured ritual murder, ritual child sacrifice, having abandoned what they must have understood – for is it not? – the ultimate propitiation, they were alone and afraid in what seemed to them a desolate land. A land . . ."

An opera hat! he thought. An opera hat, for it is *deep*, and its lining is silk, so that the cards would not adhere to it! And you can lay its crown flat, flat upon the table; and there may be myriad additional reasons, but these will suffice. *That* is the best hat!

Mars

Mars
Source: Book Two[1]

How the mind fights shy of the unexplained.

However much we must have novelty we welcome it only in its assigned place of "entertainment." To encounter it outside that precinct induces, does it not, terror.

Were one to view the night sky, starry, in the absence of the city haze, a night sky full of stars, as in the desert or the American High Plains – to see such a sky, I say, after long years of an urban life, a life empty of the Natural, might, *would* one not exclaim at the *novelty* of it?

Picture, however, a young child put to bed in his or her accustomed room, who woke, in the midst of the night, to observe, above the bed, not the room's ceiling, but, rather, that vast, whirling void, the infinite night sky.

What might that child not feel, whose mind had exhausted any possibility of encompassing this novel phenomenon?

We might, of course, picture the disordered child turning, now this way, now that, and its movements drawing the attention of the parent or adult cradling it in his arms, and the adult responding, "Hush, now, it's all right. We're only going on a sleighride to Grandmother's house," and the child sinking, once again, into a peaceful sleep.

And, as it sank down to sleep, might it not cast its gaze, once again skyward, to the spattered "dome," capable of being viewed, once again,

1 – See also The Archbishop of Kent, "Tales of Old New York," in *Shadow Puppets and the Gamelan = Indonesian Days of Love and Mystery (Beneath the Yum Yum Tree).* Notable for its complete absence of the "Missionary Position,"[A] this book is an otherwise unremarkable survey of the purported sexual practices of clergy in the employ of the British East India Company. Dull reading indeed (except for chapter 12!!!).

A – And its dust jacket (1st edn), which, when held up to the light and rotated through 90 degrees,* showed two tigers copulating.

* In either direction.

in tranquility, and appreciated as "the most novel of views." But what, you might ask, if the adult speaking, however, were not the child's parent, guardian, or care-giver? What if its voice were strange? What then, with the terror exacerbated – not the effect of an unexpected view of the stars, but of the certain knowledge one was being kidnapped?

Might the child, might the child, not, then, *long* for that other thing – that other (now viewed with nostalgia) terror-of-the-unexpected, brought about by a view of the essentially benign night sky?

Might the child, then, not profoundly (if unconsciously) wish to return to that previous "terror"?

(What an exercise in wish fulfilment the desire to "choose" one's phantasm must be! To one not caught in the nightmare of unspecified anxiety it must seem the most charming and interesting of psychologic mechanics. To one, however, being kidnapped, it would, on the contrary, be the least charming of endeavors – bemusement at the instant and autonomic formation of a psychosis to explain that which, absent the explanation, must spell psychic death.)

Or, again, let us suppose the presence by the child's side of the parent, but the parent dead, the sleigh speeding pilotless, and the infernal howling of wolves – or, again, the night sky, but this sky turning, as the parent and the child fell to earth in an aeroplane, its engine dead, and the wind whistling a protest scream, uttered on behalf of the falling.

But the psychosis, in these last moments of life, might be, might it not, a blessing – which of us can say? – for we cannot enter another's state; however much we pride ourselves upon our "empathy," the end of the day shows it to have been just another case of deluded self-love.

We know nothing of our fellows. We live and we die selfish, blind oafs, driven by hunger, fear and cold, the need to procreate, and so forth, like the other animals – but driven, also, by a counter-instinct: by the urge to utilize intelligence.

To manipulate or "control" the world around us.

Or, say, the night sky from a capsule falling through space, and the child doomed to live, and to live only, within its bounds? What greater autism? And say there was a triumph, a prodigy of will, of character, of intellect, of spirit, by which the child grew and prospered in its ethical and moral essence. To what end, finally, if all were not known "in the mind of God"?

For we were informed that everything would pass, that that dictum itself would pass from our consciousness – the memory of man – that man would pass, intelligence would pass, history would pass, the world, the universe, the totality of whatever unity within or without our capacity to name or compass it would pass. And what would remain?

No, the mind is not able to grasp it – a world-without-end – that very specter terrifying the child gazing at the sky; and, perhaps, human nature, human consciousness itself naught but a psychic scar, wrought on the brain by an electric impulse – the first, the accidental momentary, the sole vision of that sky – searing the mind, engaged, therever after, in its own unfortunate proprietary drama?

What would we know had the book not been lost?

Would we know "more" than we know now?

What do we know now?

Chip

"Who Could Describe That Scene" from *What Is Knowledge?, or The Moving Picture Boys on Mars*

The Red Planet, fourth from the Sun, that blob of flaming gas (but how we need it, how we require its heat, its light, its inspiration . . .)

Think of a traveler in the wood. Perhaps he's been out at night, perhaps he's been pursued by a bear, perhaps he's lost his way in a snowstorm, or he walked out to check on the car or something and he lost his way and he's been out all night. Maybe he was scared. Maybe he was lonely. He must of been cold.* And, maybe those phantoms of savage times (*never* far from our mind), those phantasms, those fantods, those bugaboos so progenitive of all descriptions of scholastic debate, e.g.: "Bugbears: are they racial memories, or suppressed thoughts?"; "What are we frightened of?"; "Would we be better off without our mind?", *et cetera. Any* case, there is a lot of garbage floating around in there, and it doesn't take much to set it free.

Some think that the mechanism is not "terror of the dark," "terror of loneliness," at all, but rather just deprivation of customary sensory input, which, in *itself,* is frightening, and seeks codification in that "woooo woooo" shit; or else, when *that*† is gone, the stuff we're sitting on all of the time "comes out of the woodwork."

But I don't know.

Because most times there's nothing terrifying in the dark.

It's just the closet door askew, or some loud "thump."

But in the woods, it is another story.

So mused the "chief" of all the Moving Picture Boys, "Chip."

"What cha thinking of, Chip?" Scooter said.

"Oh, nothing," Chip replied.

Reassured, Scooter leant back once again against the log and stared into the fire, the orange sparks flying up to die in the night.

"Like angels," he thought.

---

* Unless he was somewhere warm. † Customary sensory input.

"Or like devils, shooting up from Hell."

Chip settled himself down against a tree. He took the worn paperback from the thigh* pocket of his shorts, and it fell open at this spot:

"Two," or, say, not two, but some number greater than one, and less than any multiple *but* two.

But his eye was drawn not to this gibberish, but down the page, to the line drawing below.

"Why," he thought, "it is of course and obviously a vase, but when you *stare* at it, it resolves into two profiles, *vis-à-vis*. How *full* the world is!"

But when he looked up Scooter was gone.

What was that thrashing in the underbrush?

What was that cry?

What was the Purpose of Life?

The book dropped from his hands as he stood.

"The Purpose of Life . . ." he thought. "The Purpose of *Life* . . . The Purpose of Life . . ."

A strange happy light grew in his eyes as the thought formed and sought utterance in speech.

"The *Purpose* of *Life* is . . ."

The words were cut off by the embrace of the bear, squeezing Chip's chest until it cracked like a bad walnut.

The fire burnt on. The bodies were dragged away. The book lay open where it fell. There was no one to read, but had there been they would have seen this: the sub-chapter heading:

Suicide of Greind

and the notation, in a young, masculine hand,

"*Now* we're getting somewhere!!!"

* Cargo.

Mars

On the other hand, perhaps it had not come from Mars.

Perhaps it had not come from anywhere.

Perhaps the Toll Hound danced for a completely different reason.

Perhaps he did not dance at all.[1]

They asked of Jacob Cohen, "What was it before you changed it?", and, in later life, he answered, "It was different."[2]

Which it would have been had he not changed it at all.

And, on the other hand, perhaps it *had* come from Mars.[3]

How would one know – the craft of record-keeping having disintegrated to this pretty pass . . .?

But, to recur to the principal proposition, or, to "take a running start:"[4]

It was said that it was said that it must be said (or stated): all things are the case which are the case.

Under which cleansing dictum we must place "Two trains are leaving Chicago," not as the first term of a hypothesis structured as an equation, but rather as an immutable statement of fact.

O happy day, O happy universe to engender that poorest of devoirs: philosophy.

Which is to say it *could* have been Mars, and perhaps it was not; but

1 – Perhaps there was no Toll Hound, and it lived, as did the Hippogriff, but in the credulous memory of the misled, reposing there as fact – inoperative and dormant till that time it would be called into life as misinformation.
2 – From *The Living Will Envy the Dead: A Viewer's Guide to Watching the French Cinema*:

Well, what it would mean, if "everything was different"? What in the world would it mean? It would mean everything would be the same. 'N't that the thing of it? I believe it is.
3 – See *Why Did the Toll Hound Dance?* (pamphlet), op. cit.
4 – Cf. *Reculer pour mieux sauter* (Fr.).

the uncertainty of that issue may (may it not?) find counterbalance in the observation that it is true *one* of these things is true.

Thus, not unlike the focusing mechanic of a telescope, thus does philosophy, now advancing, now distancing us from a proposition, permit us that perfect, happy remove offering us peace.

O Tempura. O Morays.

Family Life on Mars

Excerpted from *Learn-to-Read*, "©"[1] "Learn-to-Read" Publication, 2122

"Florrie, Max, Bunny . . .? *Bound* over here," said Mother merrily, as she prepared their noonday snack.

"Oh John, oh *John*," she said.

"*John*," she said, in mock severity. "No! Not in front of the *children* . . ."

But the dog paid no heed, and the insistent throbbing, throbbing, throbbing of its . . .[2]

1 – The ongoing battles of the "Learn-to-Read" Foundation to secure not-for-profit status (and, so, defend its claim to copyright) would cause us to far exceed the strictures of the (Emergency) "Self-Restraint-in-Publishing Guidelines" (Tri-Lateral Commission™). Our display of the copyright bug (©) here does not constitute an endorsement by this publication of any right or prerogative on the part of the "Learn-to-Read" Foundation or of any other group. It is for this reason that it appears here[A] in inverted commas.

2 – Whence the conflation of the Martian and the Canine? It has been suggested that one link is the astronumerologic.[B] It has been suggested that previous literary allusion indicates a more venerable – no, we will not stick at saying a primordial – link between the two.[C]

A – As, of course, it does not in the original.

B – Cf. "Let's Get Sirius, or Rinty is a Dog Star", *Screenworld*, October 1938.

C – See Greind, *Shakespeare and the Toll Hound*, wherein we find:

"My dogs, Tray, Blanch, and Circumstance" (*King Lear*), by which he may have slyly alluded to Mars, being the third planet.

I will not insult the erudition of the reader by a reminder that Mars is, of course, the fourth planet, and that Greind was either an ignoramus or a fool, or was "trying to pull a fast one."

Nor shall I affront the reader's sense of the likely and possible by including the ludicrous position of Greind's apologists, to wit: that Shakespeare meant to imply *not* the "third planet from the Sun," but the "third planet from *Mercury*."

Nor shall I waste the reader's time with their endless, and fractious, and, finally, dull ratiocinations in support of their case.

Nor shall I pull the reader's ears, nor shave his belly, nor invite him out to tea, nor other caffeinated drinks. I "just don't feel like it."

Inkblots, and What Can Be Made of Them

Excerpted from Joyce Harris-Sloane, *Heroes for Sale, or The Films of Richard Barthelmess* (Winchester Press, 1961); reprinted in *The Wykemist*, fall 2026[1]

What can be made of inkblots?

Are they a message from the unconscious?

Are they a message *from the ink*?

Has too much been made of the capacity of our (the human) mind to organize the Random into Meaning? If so, whose fault is that?

And does this organization, this "new-as-organized" thing, not further complicate the problem, producing yet another bit of information* to be assimilated – as if, for all the world, a Bachelor's dissertation on "The Antecedents of the Post-Modern Novel"† were of as much worth as the Grand Canyon, or as provocative as the human capacity for mischief. No, perhaps the Japs have got it right, and the ultimate, nay, the *only* wisdom is "to refrain." For what would it profit

1 – Quoted here in the hope that it may do some good in this shithole of a world where everything is passing so quickly . . . so quickly . . . Acknowledgment(s): courtesy of *The Cousins Club*, anniversary issue,[A] "The Things You See When You're Out Without Your Gun."

A – The one known copy of this issue, discovered 2111 in a shoebox in (then American) Samoa,[A1] was itself, of course, defaced (embellished?) with an inkblot upon its cover. The shape of the inkblot arguably resembling, when inverted, the profile of Colonel House (see fig. #5) gave rise to the debate, "So What?",[A2] and, more notably, the poem, "Washrag":

Archie Butts on the *Titanic*
With his britches down
An him and Missus Strauss, jes' goin'
    to town.
Down to the bottom to prepare the way
For a good old-fashioned welcome
    for the
Lus-a-Tain-Eye-Aye.

Oh, the hush in the Forest of Argonne
And Colonel House and Woody when
    the day was won . . . [etc.]

Where ♩ = 160 (marchtime)

A1 – See *Buster Brown: The Man and the Myth* (M.P.P.), op. cit.
A2 – "Question Time," The Long House, Mon/Wed/Fri. If closed, simply drop keys in slot.

---

* Phenomena. † The "Modern Novel" presumably.

him, to've arrived at an "understanding" of the blot of ink (which understanding, after all, would have had to be, finally, subject *to* his understanding)?

And yet he stared at the page.

"Harold," the voice said. "*Harold*."

He raised his head.

"Are you coming down?"

He looked out of the window.

"Are you coming *down*, I said!"

He saw the soldiers massing. "For the last time?" he wondered.

"No," he thought. "They're going home. The whistle is that of the train returning to its peacetime life. And now the men are standing, *this last time*, under the martial discipline, before being dispersed into world without war."

He thought of the President at the (elm? black oak? marquetry?) long table at Versailles, of his grand vision of a World at Peace, of a community, a "league" of nations, allied not *against* but *for*, yes, to the contrary, *for* something.

For a proposition: that human concerns, one and all, could be addressed with humanity.

"Come down and eat, you sonofabitch," the woman screamed. "Or it's going *out*. I'm going to throw it *out*. DO YOU THINK I'M FOOLING? IS THAT THE THING? DO YOU THINK I'M KIDDING WITH YOU, AND THAT ALL I'VE GOT TO DO WITH MY DAY IS BEHAVE FOR YOUR AMUSEMENT? DO YOU THINK I FIND IT FUNNY TO SLAVE LIKE A FIELDHAND IN THIS FUCKING KITCHEN ALL DAY LONG, SO'S YOU CAN FLOP DOWN, ANY TIME YOU CHOOSE, LIKE A KING, ANY TIME YOU CHOOSE, LIKE SOME ORIENTAL POTENTATE, TO 'GRACE' ME WITH YOUR PRESENCE? YOU FAT SLOB. YOU SLUG. YOU WITLESS SLUG. I OUGHT TO'VE TOOK THE GASPIPE RATHER THAN OF HAD YOU. I COULD HAVE MADE SOMETHING OF MY LIFE. DO YOU KNOW THAT? DO YOU EVER THINK OF ME AT ALL? (*THERE*'S A JOKE), I'M TALKING TO YOU . . ."

"And yet," he read, his eyes, once again, lowered to the page, "we must of course consider the viscosity, the percentage of the undiluted solids in the ink, the 'nap,' or 'texture' of the paper . . ."

"Yes," he thought. "We must remember in our calculations that, were any in the slightest different, the resulting 'blot' would differ. Yes. Yes, yes," he reasoned. "Yes. Yes. Yes . . ."

"HAROLD, YOU *CUNT*, YOU PIG, YOU *SACK OF SHIT*," the woman screamed.

". . . but, of course, as Rorschach, as Pitou, as Bennigsen says, yes, of course, the blot must be accepted, '*per se*'; of course, but . . ."

"GET YOUR ASS *DOWN* HERE," she screamed.

He heard the sound of the drum in the freight yard.

"Yes, of course," he thought. "Like the molecules in ink, the drum 'marshals' the people now into an army, now into a mob. And they can be convened as a 'team,' as, as . . . convened, and dispersed, like atoms, like, *like* molecules, like . . ." He looked at the ink in the pot metal inkwell.

"It is a picture of possibilities, and the ink now drying in the blot(s) on the page, the image of fixity, which fixity, however, was, in being accepted as 'phenomenon' is deconstruct(ed?)(able?) again – just like the army, into component parts, each standing, just as will the demobbed 'doughboys' as irreducible phenomenon."

He heard her heavy tread upon the stairs.

Greind

Psychotic
From: *The Toll Hound*, Archives of the Academy (by permission)

> He was a true psychotic, and an artist only by courtesy.
> BURTON LASALLE,[1]
> of Greind (op. cit.)

One step forward, two steps back, one step forward, two steps back. It describes not only the progress of Humankind toward the Light, but the rhumba.

What was that fat Cuban doing with that little brown dog? Could he not learn to conduct with a *baton* like a *Christian* . . .?

Now, class, we are convened today to consider our friend, the *Flat Pass.*

It will be seen to be your job to *lure* the good, estimable Oppo, yes, *forward*, as if for the *Screen*, and, then, to scoot, as if a dog was a-nippin' at y'r heels, out five yards, and over *ten.*

Head for those sidelines, and, if it comes *your way*, get those *good hands* on it, turn upfield, and run like hell for the *uprights.*

Now let us talk about diet.

You have all heard of the *five major food groups.* I will not bore you with reiteration of their various, and, finally somewhat arbitrarily assigned characteristics. Wake *up* there, Ryzybski, wake up! *I* know how to wake him up: SEX![2] Thank you. Where was I?

1 – *The Flat Pass: A Life on the Run* (Green Bay Publications, 2002).
2 – Ryzybski wakes up.[A]

A – A transcription of Ryzybski's dream:

I was on a tall building, But I did not want to jump off. I was waiting for someone. A girl, I think.

She was late. No, *I* was late. I was late for a meeting with her. And so I thought: maybe this is why she isn't here. And then I looked down, and I saw that the whole world was under water. Then I was a fish, or something. Maybe I was an oyster, or squid, or a cuttlefish. I don't know. And then I was at work. But I'd forgotten to do something, or I'd left something back at home. My work, or something, or my homework, and then the door was stuck, and the sunlight I think it was was coming in. I tried to get up from my desk, but I couldn't because I was stuck, and the harder I tried, the worse I felt, because I felt like it was my responsibility, or something, to get up and close the door, But, if it was closed, then I couldn't see. Huh. But anyway . . .[A1]

A1 – Here the Doctor re-enters. It can be seen on the film that Ryzybski recoils, attempting to secrete the paper behind his back. He smiles at the Doctor, to indicate a lack of aggressive intent. He slinks back toward the wall, holding the paper behind him.

It was at this point an unexpected power outage caused not only darkness in the room, but the abrupt ending to the tape of the therapeutic encounter.

When the lights come back the actress playing POLLY *stands downstage arranging her wig. She looks up, as if caught in the act of primping.*

POLLY: Oh. *Hello.* They *told* me you'd be coming. It's a treat to have friends stop by. (*Pause.*) It sure gets lonely out here sometimes. (*She sighs.*) What with *Ma* away. *Golly,* I miss 'er.

(*Sound off, as if a door opening.* POLLY *reacts.*)

Huh. That'd be Mr. Black.

(*She straightens her dress. Enter* MR. BLACK, *a well-set-up middle-aged fellow in a prosperous-looking black cutaway.*)

MR BLACK: (*Looking around*) Hello, Polly. Where's your ma?

POLLY: Well, you know, Mr. Black. She's down the *village,* lookin' after Grama Wooster.

(*Pause.*)

MR BLACK: . . . then . . . we're *alone?*

POLLY: I *spose* so – course, there's *Rusty* . . .

(*She gestures off. Sound as if a dog "woofing."*)

MR BLACK: (*Distracted, as if thinking*) Yeeees . . . *quite.*

POLLY: (*Putting her hand in her pocket, revealing a white envelope*) I got the rent here, Mr. Black.

MR BLACK: . . . Mmm. (*He turns to the audience.*) *Alone,* her *Ma* in *town,* no living soul within five *miles* . . . (*He turns back to* POLLY.)

POLLY: (*Holding out the envelope*) *Here* it is!

MR BLACK: (*Taking the envelope*) *Hmm.* Yaaas. Come here, in the next room, where the *light* is better . . .

(*He ushers her offstage, as if into the "next room." And we hear a mournful, questioning "woofing," as – the curtain falls.*)

SCENE TWO

One million years later. Space.

Nebula, asteroids, space "dust" and debris stream past the windshield of the Nebula *Explorer.*

Sound, as if a dog "woofing."

The Parking Meter Problem
From: Greind, *Grundrisse*

. . . to recur to the *Parking Meter* problem,[1] beloved of twentieth-century educators, and the horror of all that era's students of philosophy. A contemporary compilation of responses[2] was a period bestseller, and graced many a rich and modest shelf.[3]

I am indebted to that rife trove of anecdotal and statistical information, and draw, *from* it, the burden of today's lecture, i.e., the (I believe, remarkable) prevalence of the response, "Raise the price of the ticket."

18% where $\Sigma = \frac{\sqrt{A/2}}{2}$ (+)(-) 5%

Cf. "Don't know," 11%; "Walk to work," 4%, and "Get fucked," at 3.5% a figure surprising even *given* the (presumably) grateful THERE IS NO ANSWER.

What sort of person, having been, in advance, so shriven, would search (presumably, so effectively) for a counter-example sufficiently provocative as to void the pre-facto absolution?

1 – A man habitually leaves his car at a parking meter some distance from his place of business. The meter requires 25 cents an hour but will accept only one quarter at a time.

The fine for letting the meter elapse is five dollars.

The man finds it inconvenient to return to feed the meter each hour during the day; and he finds the anxiety of keeping the hourly deadline in his mind onerous.

Should he overlook the hourly renewed deadline, he is almost assured to find, on returning to his car, a "ticket."

Reason suggests to him the alternative of *not* feeding the meter at all, and accepting five dollars a day as a "fee" for parking.

The man, however, frets that such behavior, although not "technically" criminal, is wrong; and that to trade rather constant (if low-level) anxiety about his parking space, for worry about his personal rectitude is a bad bargain.

What should he do?

THERE IS NO RIGHT ANSWER.

2 – *Do It* (Bogside Press, 1996).

3 – And once, in fact, secreted beneath her bodice, stopped a bullet intended for the Infanta Beatrice.

The answer may surprise:

Swedes	22%
Persons of Japanese extraction	12%
Maori	5%
etc.	

The incident, lost, of course, among the lurid "reminiscences" of incest, bestiality, sodomy, and ritual sacrifice by "Members" of the Court, is told with a style and pace sufficient to have included it (and was, in fact, discovered *in*) *Let's Write Creatively* (Scholastic Press, 1999 etc.)

What can we know of a man?

We can know his shirt size, but, though we may *infer*, we cannot even deduce from it with certitude the size of his neck.[1]

LAO TZU

1 – Quoted in *Fifty Years a Tailor, or Elohanu and Schneider,*[A] by "A Member of the Profession" (Morris K. Trotz), in which we also find:

Big hands and big feet, Ladies, big hands and big feet, and you know what *that* means . . .*

and later,

. . . or try *this*: you take the *foot* part of the *sock*, the *foot* part, mind, and wrap it around the fist. If it meets nicely, as it's wrapped around the fist, then it'll fit your foot.

And here's another one:

Take the pants – this one's for you, gents – and close the button at the waist, now wrap 'em round your neck, cause that's your waist size.

A – Cf. "The Tie," p. 197.

* Big gloves and big socks.

Binky Beaumont

Binky Beaumont

From: "Haunted Hill," *Binky Beaumont and the One Big Union*; originally, "Binky Beaumont," *The House on Haunted Hill*

Chapter Two: Those Frenchies Seek Him Everywhere

In which Ryzybski's Dream and the Mud on the Spikes are conflated with the Original Nomenclature of the Mud Pond.[1]

It was, as it must have been, a both unhappy and perceptive soul which first called that protrusion "Haunted Hill."

The name, however, having adhered to the place, what sort of man must it have been to *build* there . . .? What freak of *malheur*, anomie, depression, nay, self-loathing could have informed this otherwise incomprehensible act of situation – on the steep, inhospitable, northern slope, subject to the invariable cold north wind, and, similarly, to the drafts, vapors and miasmas issuing summer and winter from the noxious pond below?

"A true six-burner wanker," Binky said. "*That's* the sort of man . . . that's who!"

He did not realize he'd spoken aloud. His ejaculation merely the unwilled conclusion of that dialogue begun upon his first view of the spot.

"Well, no help for it!" he thought, and continued his climb.

"Aroo, aroo, arooo, aroooooo," went the dogs, chained to the faux portcullis, "aroooooooo," their teeth bared, their eyes following the progress of the solitary figure up the hill.

"Oh, stuff a *sock* in it," he thought – but did not omit to skirt that area his accomplished eye had determined as the utmost radius of that chain he hoped was to prove as stout in practice as it appeared in rest.

1 – *How Blota Got His Name, B-zine* "Commemero-Cards," series #4. See also *A Child's History of Bazoomercom.*

Clang, clang, the beasts threw themselves against their bonds, leapt, flew, *teemed* toward the approaching stranger.

"Oh, suck my *dick*," he thought, but stood still, for the moment, to assess the final certainty of the limits of their leash; and then, sanguine that, as least in so far as it concerned these beasts, he'd find no danger here, he pressed on.

Then, to the snap of the chain, and protesting animal screams of frustration, was added a third note: the crunch and *weench* of metal and masonry parting company. His eyes searched wildly for its source, which he immediately found in the ringbolt securing the dogs' lead into the wall.

To most of us forensic pathology remains a happy mystery. We are content to leave to the professional the identification of remains, etc. Who but a ghoul, in short, would occupy himself with the operations, nay, even linger in the precincts of this most grisly of endeavors?

So thought Inspecteur (Provisoire) Jean Ravigote that April day. His thoughts were interrupted by the appearance, in the antechamber of the morgue, of a tall, obviously English gentleman of middle age . . . etc.

You take it from here. (Don't forget the scouring pads.)

The Tie

"The True Meaning of Fairy Tales" or "The Mud on the Spikes" or "Low-Fat Cookery for the Ages: An Exhaustive Application of Bernoulli's Principle, Proving the Existence of God and Also Useful for Removing Gum[1] from Mohair."

A tie is like kissing your sister.

PTOLEMY THE YOUNGER, 204 BC

But a tie is more than that. Certainly it closes the collar – but a button or a stud can do the same.

And certainly it points the way down to the genitals – those organs of joy or confusion. But a tie is more – *much* more.

A tie is a statement of taste. It is proclamation not of *personality*, no, but of the individual's *understanding of his personality*. What could be more revealing? For, yes, this modern heraldry blazons not only the possessions (of wealth, of taste, of experience, in choice of cut, of fabric, of the knot itself) but of that which the inheritors of those ancient quarterings, on shield or pennon, on the lists, off on those protean conventions, the Crusades, could never have dreamed: *choice*.

[. . .][2]

. . . and what of Mars? What of that red, desiccated orb sacred to the God of War? What of it, huh? What the *fuck* of it? What's it *to* you, in this Vale of Tears?

(Pause, intervention of the Bailiff.)

Shouts of "Order."

The restitution of order.

Silence.

Passage of Time.

Death of the Dinosaurs.

1 – Chicle.

2 – Deletion or omission, running to two paragraphs.[A]

A – Based on the lacuna (= 2 inches, approx.) in the original manuscript.

Birth of Liszt.
Wrong-way Corrigan
The Transistor
The Future.[3]

. . . should we consider it a *surfactant*. But, no, I consider it an *oil*, and the hell with it.

So thought Reg Palmer, as he looked down at the empty stadium.

"They'll never know," he thought. "They'll never know."

Upon the teak desk lay the drawing, the glyph he hoped – so fervently – would be adopted as the new logo of the school he loved, the team he helped to mold, The Fighting Olympians: a pair of greaves.

"What better?" he thought; and, at the same time, "No, it will not do," which polemic was stilled (for the moment) by a third voice, that sweet voice of reason saying, "hush."

"Hush, Reg," it said. "The fault is not with the logo – the logo is fine, and beyond fine – the fault is with your *childhood*; and there's nothing you can do about that."

"Yes," he thought. "*Yes*. I must learn to take pleasure in my achievements – just as I do in my *plans* . . ."

He adjusted his tie – the school's burnt sienna, in a tight half-Windsor.

". . . this wonderful knot – named for that fornicator . . ." he thought. "But this ever has been a corrupted, sinful, world."

Below him, on the field, he saw the band – so droll in mufti – forming on the twenty-yard line.

"March on," he thought; and, "Look at that fruitcake drum major. How I would like to bend him over this same conference table, rip his corduroy pants off, and . . ."

He turned to the sound of the conference room opening.

3 – From "Washed in the Blood of the Lamb, or Seventeen Excuses for Corporate Failure," from *The Tie*:

Now it is the Future.
Now it is Not the Past.
Now it is the time of which all Dreamed.
They are gone now.
What can we make of that?
JIM BROOKS, President, Brooks Brothers

He put the smile of anticipation on his face; but saw not the expected kindly visage of President Wilson, no, but a shape, a form; he could not force his mind to interpret it as a "being," no, not yet – it was for him, in this first instant of contact, nothing but a swirling, inchoate mass of – tentacles? limbs? What, *shapes*, finally, and he thought, "Oh, that's just a . . ." And it was only then, only now when his quick, his inventive mind, taxed to the uttermost, could offer no completion to the thought that terror set in.

His last thought, before he disappeared into its maw, was "Mars."

And what of the Mud on the Spikes?

Binky Beaumont, Greind [Bennigsen] and Ryzybski were of course "The Three Men" to whom the Fantasist alluded.[1]

1 – And it was *this* "prediction" which inaugurated the inclusion in the Liturgy of "How *could he have known* . . . How could he have *known* . . .", Canonical Authority, "Three men will surely follow me", Canto XXXVII: 4.21. Cf. Bill McCloskey and the "After-Hours Boys," "Tom, Dick, and Harry," from *A Child's Christmas on Mars* – all proceeds donated to Kamp Kawaga,[A] fresh-air camps of Mare Nostrum.

A – Such of course, when proved not to be the case, occasioned the defenestration of Mr. McCloskey and the resultant closing of Madison Avenue (N.Y.) between 33rd and 34th Streets, which, if it did not inaugurate, certainly exacerbated the confusion and the terror of "That Day."

The Capsule

In the Capsule

Jacob Cohen, University of Southern Wilson,
New South Mars

. . . these psychiatrists, psychologists, psycho-orthographers, and "just-plain-psychos," who thought they could adduce the existence of the soul from that "one word" in the thirteenth session.

Well, we all know what became of *them*.

But what (after the derision) became of their argument? That is the question the Old Wrangler raised; and it was, of course, for that that he was exiled.[1]

His production, in the "exile" years is irretrievably lost to us.[2]

It remains to attempt to determine the content and scope of his revelations (for revelations they most assuredly were)[3] from his movements.

Starting with his first remove (i.e. starting from Media, P.A.), let us draw a line to Boise. Let us now intersect it at the Golden Mean, leaving the bulk of the line to our left (or the west), and draw a perpendicular of equal length, itself bisected by the Media–Boise line, we find, at this line's northern terminus, Ottawa, and, at the south, a point in the Gulf of Mexico 200 miles SSW from Tampa, Florida: THE POINT PREDICTED FOR THE CAPSULE'S RE-ENTRY!

Are you surprised? Are you overcome? Well: *welcome to the club!*

For it is not simply a "Christian" outlook, to "find a meaning in things." It is not, as has been (unsportingly) suggested, a "survival" of "The Great Chain of Being," no, it is *the nature of the world*. And it was

1 – See *The Old Wrangler in Burbank* (privately printed).

2 – From: Will and Ariel Durant, on *Our Boardinghouse* (NBC Radio: Blue Network, 12 June 1939):

QUESTION: Is anything ever "irretrievably lost"?
ANSWER: Well, if not, where is my other sock!

3 – Look at the photos. You can see it in his eyes. *That* man had been around the block.

this that the Old Wrangler knew, *this* which was the cause of his exile, and *this* which he, *in his very peregrinations*, strove to communicate to us, and *this* is why I have chosen him as the subject of my paper.

Relics
In which is discussed the notion of the Capsule as a reliquary

The Stoics said, "Who rides, decides." The sentiment reappears in the Time of the Riots (or, as it was known in the period afterward, "in those days"): "Whatever gets you off."[1]

That which, in this case, "gets us off," dear Reader, is the issue of the Capsule *qua* reliquary.

It is not enough, I feel, to aver to those (granted, widespread) instances of "the Death in Life." The literature of the submariner, the miner, and this author's first marriage furnish instances abundant of the same.

And, indeed, nowhere are they lacking. It was Ralph Waldo Emerson himself who said, more than once, that "most men lead lives of quiet desperation."

Now, the cases of the submarine explorer, the luckless astronaut, *et cetera*, granted, "raise the stakes." In these the issue is not "how many times a week is it healthy or normal to have sex?" but whether or not one can expire gracefully in the absence not only of water, food and air, but of an audience, an overseeing power, or its ideation, for whose benefit or, at the least, in whose sight, or in the light of the idea of which, the display or impersonation of stoical dignity might give, to the sufferer, if not a philosophic mitigation of the throes of death, at least an interest in the progress of those throes which, absent other diversion, might be enjoyed as entertainment. Many, I say (aping Emerson), lead lives *et cetera*. But *few* have the site of those lives turned into a "dime museum."[2]

1 – This seeming vacuism achieved, in the decades following the Riots, the invocational, placative, apotropaic statis of "Cosa da Inquisition" (see Abbot Encastellaugh, *The Spanish Inquisition:* 14??–189?, *or ¿Quien es la sobre prima?*[A]

2 – See Mrs. Lida Parker Knowles, and the Ladies of the Church Committee, *Memories of Old Pasadena* (*feuilleton*).

A – This note is spurious.

What is gained, finally, by what may be not only a factitious presentation – contrived through its very recourse to the dramatic – but a factitious presentation *of a spurious article.*

For the presentation of the artefact, though it would seem to improve if not supplant the experience of the historical, and, so, intellectual, and, so, metaphysical, and, so, moot, with the experience of the actual,[3] in fact can engender, at its *optimum*, not "understanding," but *belief.*

For must one not exercise belief in the authenticity of the objects displayed in order to undergo that thrill which, the candid must admit, is the whole point of the exercise?

It is my thesis that this *tressaillement* comes not from proximity to the historic real, but as a chemic, glandular result of our own self-exaltation – of the exercise of our power to endorse, of our "belief."

What can it mean that Krautz, or Jacob Cohen, what could it mean if the Old Wrangler himself saw or sat inside the Capsule?

It could mean no more than that this or that writer, recognized as an "authority" (by, of necessity, no one more exalted than "another writer") *proclaimed* such to've occurred.

And why should we presume in our historians a skill or veracity greater than that discovered in the average of any trade, group, coven, or profession?

Well, then, what are those people *looking* at? Who is to say it *is* the Capsule? Who is to say those *are* the Books?

And though I am not the first, I yield to no one my pride of place in being the most vehement in proclaiming that the *true locus* of the Capsule is *not* (*pace* the writers of greeting cards) "on the Mall," but in the Mind.

3 – Cf. *The Gnostic Union with "the Real"*, op. cit., and Carl Young, *Fantasist and Fantasy.*

Folderol

Folderol
or: "In Defence of Bennigsen" by "Praetor"

Yes, they had translated it as "folle de roi," and thought themselves beyond reproach (though who might have reproached them is beyond this writer's understanding) (with the blatant exception, of course, of this writer himself) (and thus, perhaps, they weren't so crazy after all) (on *that* point).

How like, then, the academic mind to strive "to make a showing," rather than "to show the truth." For, to that mind, that sloppy, lazy, weak, co-opted, hypocritic, self-ignorant, destructive, non-accountable, finally craven, mis-marriage of synapses, there *is* no truth, no truth save: Get through the hour; and: Keep your job. For how dare they, those "professors" of the Romance tongue, those soi-disant philologists, sprung or appointed as by fell parthenogenesis, from the gross Body of Their Own, how *dare* they count their work "done," or "exhaustive," or, in fine, apply to it any adjective indicating a worthy or successful completion, when they'd overlooked the blatant, glaring, obvious, the essential progression.

For, *if* folderol to *folle de roi*; then, of necessity (the merest amateur of Scrabble(r) could see it), *folle de roi*, in a retrograde intuition,[1] into *foi de roi*.

For, was it not the *faith* of Louis Onze, who sent Priedieux (and, thus, his dogs) (and, thus, Bienguele) into Louisiana?

No, it was not his *folly*, but his *faith* which sent them there.

Faith, I say, which has the power to move men, mountains, *bowels*,[2] and that about covers it.

1 – "Intuition" is perhaps much too strong a term. I would suggest the alternative "observation," or some other word which indicates just looking at the damn thing and seeing the obvious.

2 – See the works of C. F. Post, Battle Creek, Michigan (www./po-toastie; fee involved), and *Whippies*, op. cit.

The Sun shone down
The Moon shone down
The Eyes of the Soul-Sick Loon shone down
The Wrath of The Almighty soon thrown down
Upon Louisiana.

A. LOMAX, *Bayou Days 'n' Ways*, Library of Congress
(reconstructed from "The Stop 'n' Shop," 2111, © the Editors of *Vogue*)

And here we find a sly allusion to the source of the King's faith. (Or, better, we might say, the "catalytic moment,"[3] for who can say what is the source of his (or anyone's) faith? As it is, or as we perceive it as* a "recognition," must we not say that it (the faith) was "there all the time" – that it is "immanent,"† that it, perhaps, is neither a "hint," nor a "memory" of God, or the Godhead, but that it is God HimSelf? And that that's why we like it?

(Let us say, therefore, rather, "an important moment in the King's spiritual development".) It (the verse) refers to the King's revelation at the telescope, the references to the Sun and the Moon being rather clear, the soul-sick Loon referring to the King himself,[4] the "Wrath of The Almighty" being, of course, the *grand mal* to which the King was famously subject; thus, "upon Louisiana" leaping into stark relief as "Upon Louis Onze."

How thrilling, how dear, how sweet, that seventeenth-century French ditty survived in the New World, in the Bayou songs, as a (not unpleasant) nonsense rhyme, which, *though all its singers were supposedly ignorant* of the King's "revelation," and the part played therein by Botté (his épagneul de Bretagne), became part of the ritual of the tolling party, and, in fact, was first anthologized in the Modern Era in *The Song of the Toll Hound*.[5]

CAN THIS BE CHANCE?

3 – Carl Rogers, *The Devil Made Me Do It.*
4 – The original, of course, referring not to the waterbird (genus *gavia*), but to the King, employing the Middle English *lauen* (from the Icelandic, meaning, "one who is at the end of his rope"). Cf. Jespersen's (attempted) conflation of the Althabascan ⅃∧˥∧ and the Norse. I would remind him (were he here to remind) that the Vikings sailed *west*. Duh.
5 – *Songs of the Rod 'n' Gun* (privately printed).

* The same thing. † Whatever that means.

And, to those answering in the affirmative, then, what *is* chance?

I propose that it is a process, or event beyond your understanding which you, in your ignorance, have enshrined as being incapable but of remaining so.

Note on "Folderol"[6]
Found in the Capsule

The *grand mal* / revelation at the telescope / Priedieux dispatched to Louisiana. *Why?*

These are the three (major) areas of (academic) investigation in "Folderol."

It has always baffled this investigator that the student mind has overlooked *completely* that area which I, for one, believe would offer, if not an explanation, at least a satisfying avenue of *exploration* – that of the antiquary.

For, it has been noted that in that time there were to be found, both in Old and New France, and in the immediate areas of Priedieux perambulation, *pieces of furniture which bore his name.* I offer it not as a "suggestion," to those students named above. Merely as an observation.

6 – This is an example of that "academic humour" to which we, in honesty, must admit Greind was partial.

The three areas – the *grand mal*, the revelation, Priedieux's decampment – constitute, of course (in *petit*) the syllabus of that year's study at the Institute. It is not for the student to "choose," but to apply him- or herself to the entire course of study. And Chet's faux-avuncular "aside" must be seen as what it was: a ploy, and the operation of a sick, sick mind. For those students who accepted his "suggestion" and wrote on the priedieux were failed, dropped from the university, and, thus, debarred from an academic life.[A]

How sad is the misuse of power.

Lord Acton said that power corrupts, and that absolute power corrupts absolutely.[B]

His success with the *bon mot* betrayed him into that unfortunate and touching waste of what promised to be both a brilliant diplomatic career, and a rather nice life; for, having uttered that most famous line,[C] he could never afterward utter a simple statement, but it had to be (to his mind) pithy, weighty, memorable, and rhythmic.

A – The author fails to find significant the fact that two of them were killed. Hmm.

B – *The Sayings of Lord Acton* (Ridgely, Hants: Beaverboard Press).

C – Christmas Panto, London 1912.

Questions ranging from "How are you, Binky?" to "Would you like the scrod?" were met with a tilt of his head, a sad, knowing look, a sigh, and the rendition of a one-liner aspiring to universal applicability.

No wonder his wife shot him.

But, to return, how sad is the misuse of power. And how pathetic the autonomic operations of our human breed.

Having subdued the beasts, harnessed first fire, then water,[D] then the electron, the atom, the neutrino, muuguu, and starlight itself, where do we end, who know no boundaries nor cess? Where do we end but, time after time and inevitably, in the shit-hole, warming fire giving way to instruments of war, wisdom to academia; for, the one aspect of the inevitable we may decry all day is that it's bound to happen. [*The manuscript here continues in holograph:*] And it won't change a goddamn thing.

D – Cf. Archimedes, in *Roman Holiday*, directed by William Wyler (1953).

Quick Study Guide

See also: "The Sample Paragraph," p. 81.
(The third term is lost.)

EAST led with a reference disallowed as "literary," which his opponents, erroneously, interpreted as "signaling," and responded to, accordingly, as below:

SOUTH Pass.
WEST Pass.
NORTH Pass. (!!!!!)

Any rational consideration of NORTH's response must pale, and its proponent retire in awe at the outcome of what could (and, the result aside, can and must) be seen as a monstrous, an inexplicable blunder, if not, as a craven capitulation or surrender, a cheap resignation hoping to escape detection in its guise of thoughtlessness, or inattention.

Of what, we ask, could Greind have been thinking? And we would not have been alone. Had one been in the audience at the announcement, one would have seen this: first, general irritation, and the approach of several onlookers to the Marker, asking that the obviously erroneous notation of NORTH's move be corrected; second: incredulity – as the audience conferred with one another in an attempt to obtain that natural explanation which each, then, found was not to come; lastly: rage.

But while the audience raged, play continued. With the sequelae far too well documented to require inclusion here.

The question remains: Was EAST signaling? And, if not, what the *hell* did he think he was doing?[1]

This and like inquiry was stilled, of course. In the days following,

1 – The chances of a victorious outcome for the Blue team, subsequent to the bidding above, have been calculated as one in 2^{35}.

the Blue team returned to Mars, and the Greens had, in defeat, surrendered their platform.

It remained for the scholarly community to "pick up the ball and run with it."[2]

Which, indeed, and famously, in the first years following the Riots (R + 6 → R + 120), they did.

But not before the issue had been mooted by the Arts.

I call the reader's attention to Greind's "The New Palio," composed, we are told, while the dust was still (literally) settling in what had been the streets:

Yes, and Yes, Again,
Who rested at The Table,
Eyes locked in a gaze
Which spoke of Intelligence
SO ABRUPT as to Discomfit Wilson.
"To Wit, To Woo"
"Pass." Yes, and "pass" again –
Ye Ancient Geeks,
Who fashioned Drama,
Look down and gape
At the appearance of
This Bright, New Thing.

He goes on to delineate the various inabilities of the Ancient Geeks, to "grasp," to "digest," to "render usable" (meaning, we must assume, to "turn into Art").

This upset, this event, which (he opines) carries within itself all the aspects of Art, rendering further elaboration pointless.

This would seem to be a celebration, by Greind, of Art, and, by extension, of the Artist. However, it is quite another thing. In severing the, one would have thought, not only necessary but necessarily casual relationship between Artist and Art, Greind lauds, not the Deity, or Chance, if you will, but the *Critic* – i.e., that force capable of

2 – See Ryzybski's Dream. (And cf. Ryzybski's Dream, pp. 187–8.)

recognizing "Art" in, we may say, "random," er, perhaps, better, in that, in a phrase of the day, "untouched by human hands."

And in this he begs the issue. If the issue is, as I hold it to be, "signaling."

Let us return the cursor "*ad initium*."

Are there doors, some door, *Man* was not meant to open?

"No," thought Ginger, as she laid the book down. "No. Nor woman, too."

"What are you reading, Hon?" Chet said, as he came in.

"Oh, nothing."

The Inner Code

The Inner Code

Much has, unfortunately, been written about the "Inner Code," conflating such (should it have existed, which this writer, for one, must deny) with the Joke Code – as if the Joke Code were (as was, as popular opinion held, the "Inner Code") a cereal-box competition. Granted, yes, the Vedas, Sutras, *et cetera ad nauseam*, the apocrypha, arcana, and all similar "hid," "inner," or "infra-" canons partake or aspire to partake of that merit ascribed to the "lowly," whence, the philosophically mature have long been wont to opine, comes wisdom. But their very age, their time-in-rank, so to say, as it adds status, weight, or, as the Ancients had it, "believability" to their position, simultaneously attenuates any claim they may possess of being undiscovered, "low," "poor-in-spirit," bullshit, and so on.

Unfortunately,* it is not only religions which attract, inveigle and entrap by their claims to simplicity. We all are attracted to the undiscovered. In it we find that titillation of "something-for-nothing," whether in real estate, in exploration, science,[1] engineering – the attraction of each and all may be reduced to that sympathetic excitation of the quintessential human survival mechanism: the ability to imagine a way of getting out of work. Now, this work-to-be-avoided may be the inspiration for the center-span bridge (an alternative preferable to the wet trudge or long row from one shore to the other), or in a religious Epiphany ("I don't have to worry any more!"), but all and each please, attract and excite as they employ the core, and irreducible essence, of our human being.

How this spark has driven and has aided us! Without it we were, long ago, part of the compost on that moldering orb of our birth; it gave us medicine, sport, literature, art, and science. How could we

1 – J. M. Potts, M.D., Martian Space Service, *I Found the Cure for the Salk Vaccine.*

---

* For the seeker-after-truth.

have hoped that it would be an unmixed blessing? And, who, then, are we to carp at the unfortunate but arguably corollary creation of condensed books and the evening news?

For there *was*, of course, no "Inner Code." The suggestion of the same was but a ploy (as has been exhaustively demonstrated elsewhere)[2] to market Whippies. And those obtuse enough to've "sent their boxtops in," found out the same.

They underwent that painful and humiliating revelation. Faced with their error, they had to stand, in light of day, and admit to themselves that their intellect had availed them nothing and they (a) had been "had," and (b) had no one to blame but themselves.

Would that the academics had had the courage to "stand the gaff" of a similar self-revelation.

For it is in this, I believe, that lies the difference between those who wear the cap and gown and human beings.

The very structure of the advertisement reveals and must reveal it to all but the most inverted as a joke:

Two trains are leaving Chicago, as young Billy and young Sue arrange their picture puzzle on the small folding table.[3]

Where, I ask in exasperation, where in these twenty exhaustively plumbed, studied, deconstructed, *re*constructed, perused, parsed, and analyzed words, is it *implied*, let alone stated, that Billy and Sue are on a train?

Or that they are in (or have just left) Chicago? Where? *Point* to it. It's a joke. The problem is a *joke*. IT'S A JOKE, PEOPLE!

It was perpetrated by the folks at Whippies, and there *was* no answer.

HOW COULD THERE BE? THEY WERE NOT ON A TRAIN!

Where is it written?

The contest was the construction of an idle or mischievous hour at the advertising agency.

2 – "Donna and Chet", in *La Nouvelle Ecosse: Pays des Vacances exquises* (Editions Vuillard).
3 – "A History of Whippies," International Pâtisserie (formerly Ceres) Archives.

They. Were. Not. On. A. Train. *If* they were not, then, is no connection to the Joke Code, and, then, generations of mush, written on the "Inner Code," are worthless* trash.

Tesso, the fifteenth-century Japanese swordmaster, admonished his students that there was no inner meaning to the strokes, the point was "just to cut the other guy's head off."

Those occupying themselves in contemplation of the "meaning" of "three petals falling"[4] missed the whole point. They were "a bunch of assholes,"[5] and had they gotten in an actual dust-up, they, inevitably, must have come up wanting, for they were missing the point.

Just so those searching for the Inner Code.

There is no Inner Code.[6]

A Note on "The Inner Code"

The editor's statement that "this assumption was never investigated" is, of course, nonsense. And we, at our "wise, nay, infallible remove"[7] now, of course, know that not only were Billy and Sue on a train, but that the train was, in fact, one of two leaving Chicago; and we are, further, of course, aware not only of the intended destination, but of the actual end of the "other train," that train known to generations of schoolchildren as "train B":[8] the train which carried Greind.

It was, ironically, his *Tales of the Old Wrangler*[9] which gave rise to the anti-Gnosticism of the late twenty-first-century Nominalists, whose influence is seen so clearly in the fragment above.

Taking a calm overview one can understand, and can, perhaps, almost "feel" the anxiety which gave rise to their spiritual and intellectual retrenchments.

4 – A cut toward the knee.
5 – Tesso.
6 – It should be noted that even if there is no Inner Code, those responding to the Whippies ad ("Win a free membership in the Bootsie Club") did constitute a mailing list; and it was from this list that the first subscribers of *Bongazine* came. Wheels within wheels.
7 – *Lettres de mon Moulin.*
8 – © Scholastic Testing Service.
9 – See extract below.

* And, for the most part, ill-written.

We cannot, however, condone nor excuse their actions.

Their "sticks and stones both can and shall break their bones"[10] has justly earned for its authors both a niche in history and a place in the language.

From: "Tales of the Old Wrangler"

Clip clop, clip clop, clip clop.

How these sounds echo, not only *per se*, but, rendered through the necessarily traductive operations of language as a not-only-heard, but half-*spoken* (in what reflection must dismiss as a grossly anthropomorphistic predisposition) phrase.

No. No, however they may be (however inaccurately, at the end of the day) reduced and approximated by the alphabet, and, so, capable of being transcribed, and, thus, communicated and repeated, they (the sounds) are not the letters which approximate them; and the letters themselves, retronumically, and our reliance upon them, dilute and destroy our ability to hear the sounds pure, in themselves.

Clip clop, clip clop went the donkey's hoofs, and "Whoa, there, Chico!" Chet called out. For he had been roused from his semantic reverie by another sound, a sound which was not rendered into "words," a sound which he perceived, and upon which he acted, but which was of a nature so pressing, so exigent, he did not pause to perceive that he perceived it, nor that he had spoken, nor upon his subsequent immediate movement.

For his body knew its meaning, which meaning struck beyond the lenses of intellect and straight to the cerebral cortex, to his innermost, most animal core. And he was acting on it before he was aware that he had heard it at all. It was the click of a revolver's hammer being drawn back to full-cock.

"Well, *that* knocked my dick in the dirt," Chet thought, as he crawled to cover behind the boulder at the side of the road. "Some mucho mal hombre ahead, fix'n to *bushwhack* me," he thought, and chuckled. "Wall, *lessee* about that!"

10 – "Fee fie fo fum," *Bongazine*, vol. xv no. 10.

The burro stood where Chet had left him, in the middle of the road. Chet heard him paw the ground absently.* He slowly and quietly drew his boots off. He rose and worked his way, silently, around the boulder. He drew the large bowie knife from the sheath which hung down his back, and moved around the rock.[11]

11 – I would have liked to've been there.

* No comment.

Aphrodite

Or: "The Inner Code as Mariolatry"[1]
Lost note from *Lady of Spain*

Imagine the chagrin of the archeologists, toiling away, day after day on the *et cetera*, only to have the son of a bearer bring into camp the *Shard*, in which, *et cetera, et cetera* . . .

The narrative breaks off here, and resumes with the point of the whole thing, to wit: the third (disputed) strophe,[2] that is:

Lady of Spain, you big whore, you . . .

Compare "Aphrodite in her see-through nightie,"* in the poem "Two Bits and Dear at That," by Eugene Fields, from *Old Chicago Days, or The Algonquian Confederacy: More Than Just a Bunch of Indians*, from which collection I include the following:

Cho-tan-nah-pah
chewed her moccasins until
they were soft as the
whispered response of
a sex-crazed fourteen-year-old
latterly giv'n in marriage . . .

Why is this doggerel included?

If we take every seventeenth letter in the poem we find this: DFSS, etc., a near-perfect recapitulation of that cryptogram[3] written in

1 – In the original, *mis*-spelled as "Martiality," and, therefore, mis-filed, an orphan, with an orphan's brave face masking but never concealing self-doubt, fear, and a general sense of unfairness, in the section "Mars."
2 – "Lady of Spain": (a) I adore you [pull down your pants]; (b) I'll explore you.
3 – Was it a simple error in transcription, in arithmetic, which led Greind to his (mis)identification of the two cryptograms?

* Nighty.

Mrs. Wilson's urine,[4] and tossed through the library window, and, thence, into our hearts.

The "Algonquian" series ends, it will be seen, with the *sixteenth* letter.

It is only through an act of sophistry that the identity can be postulated.

Question: Is this an arithmetic or ethical error? Let us examine it.

The human wish to find connections has betrayed us into calamities far worse, far more destructive than this. But it is not, I fear, a solecism to suggest that we may, in this arguably benign case, perceive [*sic*] the paradigm.

Note

From: *It's Beyond Bearing*, episode 12: "Historical Anomalies and the Insupportable Weight of Coincidence" (Pan American Museum of Broadcasting)

This beggars imagination. The effort to find meaning in this academic nonsense exhausts the creative and moral capacities of anyone not seeking tenure. How long must we put up with this shit? Are we, like Frank Sinatra, destined to live *for ever*?

Are we, like the sea anemones, born but to live, immobile, swaying now this way, now that, in the most circumscribed of orbits, glued to a rock in this undulating sea of *shit*, this precious, casuistic, useless crap, this *vomit*, this scholastic and obscene perversion of all that is good?

Will no one answer me? Am I *alone*?

4 – The *urine* was Mrs. Wilson's,[A] *but did she pen the note*?

The ancient joke, of course, is "Mr. President, someone has written 'Fuck Nixon [Truman, Disraeli, Leon Blum, Frederick of Prussia, Pharaoh]' in urine in the snow. We've analyzed the urine, and it is that of your wife. Worse news, still, the handwriting is that of your Prime Minister." Ancient joke, still good today. Just change the names.

A – "Chemical Analysis of Urine: The Wilson Note", Report of the Bureau of Investigation (later, the Federal Bureau of Investigation).

(I am indebted, also, to Herbert Yardley's immortal *Secrets of the American Black Chamber*, for acting as a shim and holding up one corner of my work table during the writing of this piece. I would also like to thank my wife, Boo, for her unending good sense, good humor, and generosity, and my three girls for their patience. Daddy loves you very much.)

The Timesheets

The Timesheets: A Timely Surprise

An interpolation – "The Events of That Day" – from *Lais of the Fantasist*

As we here deviate from the traditional arrangement[1] it is perhaps not inappropriate[2] to improve upon the unexpected intermission with the injection of an "olio."

To begin: may we not address that phrase, so oft used as to've become (a) part of the language, and (b) wellnigh invisible: "these few slim volumes." To what did this originally refer?

Most would immediately respond "the Diaries" – but they are wrong.

The phrase, though first penned by their "discoverer," refers not to the Diaries, but to the, to him, far more precious artefacts, the *Timesheets*.

Did Krauz (*fils*), indeed, *have* access to the Timesheets, you may riposte, and would, in so doing, place and mark yourself as belonging to the mainstream of Traditional Exegetic Thought.

He did.

"Defend your thesis," you respond.

I will.

Let us cast our imaginations back to the Mud Pond, in that period *directly* before it received its name.

I will ask you to picture ducks, geese, swallows, the occasional coot or "grebe," a "loon," perhaps, if this is not to overtax your imagination, the odd rowboat, skiff or dory, a green slime upon the water's surface which, in my youth, was known as "whale vomit," but which is, of course, *algae*. Reeds you may, in your mind's eye, find along the marge, which merge, as we mount up the bank, into a dense grass skirting

1 – In the original, "cantillations".
2 – Shouts from the floor: "Oh, *bullshit*."

what is now the Mall. We see a man's face, gazing, to the east, over the pond, in his hand a magazine or "book."[3]

I now ask you to review (not to *question*, never to *question*, solely to *review*) the Events of That Day – freely, easily, as they come to you. The Coffee and Roll; the Lady who was so Rude; the Bus and the Bus Transfer; the odd cast of the sky; the gate; the Timeclock; the Second Cup . . .

Now, hold this thought for one brief moment:

I have recited to myself all the Events
as they transpired on That Day.

What is that "nagging" feeling?[4]

3 – Traditionally, of course, *Bongazine*, vol. 1 no. 1, or, in the case of the Traduction, *Dink Stover at Yale.*

4 – Here, once again, as the narrative breaks off, I must recur to the Schedule of Medications, in the hope that, if it does not clarify, it may aid the reader to pass the time until his or her next meal, job, promotion, extramarital affair, insight, sleep, *et cetera, et cetera, moo moo moo moo moo n'jambaya. R'koo, r'koo, r'koo.*[A]

A – Transcribed from the best available (existing and enhanced) record(ing)(s); cf. The Diorama: "Martian Landings in Song and Story on The Mall" – "The Shame of the Smithsonian," J. Dilinger.

Ages – Sages

The *Motive-Valise* explored[1]

> That is a question for the Sages.
> That is the Question of the Ages.
> (Found in a trunk in Pinsk)

"He said that he's prepared, at any moment, to make an impassioned plea for whichever side of the argument inevitably proved to have been wrong."

"How frank," the Proctor replied, and went on about an *obiter dictum* of his own, concerning the heat of a summer's day and the – in retrospect – quite charming insect life associated with it in his mind.

"The fellow's stuck in the pre-sexual," thought Greind, as the man droned on, not unlike, it may have occurred to him, those dragonflies, bees, or whatever on the marge of that cold lake.

"F'the lake was so cold, why'd they have the insects?" he wondered.

The man continued about the dog which had been at his side.

"Long dead," thought Greind, "long dead. Necessarily long dead, for their life span is a fraction of our own, all things being equal, and it would be seen as obscenity, were they to live as long as we. And yet," he thought, "we pine to hang around for ever, like some deep-sea tortoise, rumored to wade through the centuries."

". . . which bring you to us *today*," said the Proctor.

"Yes," Greind said.

They stared, one at the other, for the longest time.

"Whoever talks first loses," Greind thought. And then he thought of a young girl, who, at the time, seemed to him as a quite nice young girl,

1 – "Can it be, may it be, *can* it be that no one has remarked the coincidence of the 'Trunk' motif in the canon with – and proven through statistical analysis to fall *exactly* in a pattern 1:4:5:1 with – the 'Bootsie' material? Can I be the first to conflate the American 'Trunk' with the British 'Boot'? What joy!" Krautz.[A]

A – Disallowed, as composed under the influence of steroids.

but who, at this remove, he realized must have been a stunning vision of nubility.

"Or, to put it differently," he thought, "must *now* be seen to be, to one at this age – to myself, in fact – or, to put it better, to have been *some stunning piece of ass*. (Although, at that age, she was, to me, just 'some girl.')"

The other spoke. "You know," he said, "I was telling you about my *dog* . . ."

"Wait wait wait," Greind thought. "Have you never heard of 'a companionable silence'?"

". . . as if he *knew*, before I *spoke*," the man said.

"Well, tell me how he would of known more *afterwards*," Greind thought. "I mean, for Christ's sake, he was a *dog*."

". . . to get the *paper*, or . . ."

"And I especially remember," Greind thought, "(oh, how I'd like to see that *now*) that space, that truncated triangle, if you will, at the top of her thighs, and below the pubis. *You could see light there!*"

" . . . or, when I was sad, *he*'d be sad," the man went on.

Greind looked at him with a contempt unmixed with pity.

The above is, of course, a mediocre example of the genre. That it is fiction need not, I feel, be decried. There exist various examples of the genre worthy of consideration, if not as literature, then, at least, as reasonable specimens of entertainment. That it treats of an historical figure, again, need not in any way disqualify it from a (granted, unsubstantiated) claim upon our respect and attention. Greind (Bennigsen), for good or ill, "belongs to us all."[2]

But I must object, as, I am sure, must any fair-minded reader, to the arbitrary inclusion, and the disrespect which impartial analysis fails to find absent, in the inclusion, I say, of the character of *the dog* – *the dog*, dragged in by the heels* in what we can only consider a (feeble) attempt to enliven an otherwise barren, mechanical, and pointless interchange.

I do not mean to endorse the jingoistic "if it was in the Capsule

2 – Cf. *Terra Incognita, or Find Your Way Home* (Floorsgaarrd, Sweden: Silva Compass Company).

---

* Hocks.

it was good enough for me" and have long vociferously opposed that school of – we cannot call it "thought", for we must call it "politics." But I find myself driven *into their arms* by productions of this ilk. I swear to God I do.

Slowly I Turned
or: *Thoughts on the Spit*, by St. Athanasios[1]

How do these new discoveries[2] affect our view of the world – for it must be the merest craven who'd deny it. Fire, the repudiation of a geocentric cosmos, TV, life on Mars, each, in its way, each in its day, changed, *formed* the life of Man.

What are we, anyway, we lying, evil worms – infecting this green sphere first with our thoughts, then with our words, and lastly with our deeds?

What are we but a disastrous failed experiment? Nothing, really; or, at the most, not very much at all.

How infinitely preferable the monastic life – a round of contemplation, and occasional oral or anal sex.[3]

How, if not noble, if not blameless, then we will say, more worthy of emulation, to move over the world not like the sea, no, pulling, filling, ebbing, forcing, no, but like the wind, or wind-over-the-sand, or *gentle* wind-over-the-sand (for the sirocco or harsh desert wind *does* have the power to affect, to alter, to engender, passions, if, for nothing else, for *shelter*, for, while it does blow unceasingly, week after week, one wishes, one comes to wish that one were dead – or, at least, in a less sandy place).

And what has altered, since the Capsule returned?

Is it the fact of life on Mars which alters all?

No. No more than would a like announcement concerning Zabia, Kansas, or somewhere else.

No. It is the revelation, as it must be, of that life's quality which must, which doth, which shall inform all human thought and action for the next foreseeable while.

1 – Disputed. ("For the books, do you see, for the books were found on the Shelf, and, so, must be considered.")
2 – Nobody has any idea what he is talking about.
3 – cf. "How About It?", A. Huysmans.

Muuguu

From Tales of the Fantasist

This, do you see, *this* is the Essence of Muuguu. Not "to do," not "to be," but, rather, to neither "do," nor "be."

This is not "of the essence." This *is* the essence. This is *it*. A lot of jagoffs are running around, spewing out this or that absurd nonsense; no doubt, some of 'em are (or think they are) in earnest. Big Deal.

That is not our look-out.

All you can do: stick "close to the *Thing*," and Keep your Head Down. Go with God.

You'd have to go in *any* case.

You don't have to go home, but you Can't Stay Here.

This is the Essence of Muuguu.[1]

1 – When I was a little boy I had a puppy. I miss him.

Lola Montez and
the Moving Picture Boys

Lola Montez

(Often conflated with J. of T., her effigy still exhibited on "Capsule Day," Papua, New Guinea)[1]

It was said that Lola Montez died in agony, after drinking an over-the-counter preparation warranted to stave off sexual debility. The deeper question: did Lola Montez ever live; and, the ancillary query: if so, what was that dog on her lap in the linecut (*London Illustrated Times*, vol. 81 no. 6)?

Granted it has been identified as a King Charles Spaniel, but it must take an act of either faith or intellectual dishonesty to overlook the extensive delineatory gifts of the engraver *in re*: face and form, textile and décor, and to suggest his muse failed him only in the matter of the dog.

Why?

No, we must aver that the drawing is an accurate rendition of *something*. Of what?

To answer the question, we must look to the skies.[2]

1 – See *Lola Montez and the Cargo Cults* [?*Cunts*], Yale University Press; *Boston Blackie Meets His Match*, op. cit.

2 – It is obvious that the author here intended, once again, to mount his hobbyhouse and "quirt" it into a lather; or, to put it simply, to discommode us once again with his beloved theory of Spontaneous Appearance, or of Synchronicity between this world and space,[A] this particular anecdotal snippet of coincidence: the resemblance between the beast on Montez's lap and that creature whose likeness was found scratched into the *exterior* of the Capsule.

QUESTION: HOW WE GO ASTRAY AFTER THE "EVIDENCE" OF OUR SENSES

Love, politics, commerce, war – search in vain to find a theater of endeavor not replete with blatant instances of self-deceit. What can we not convince ourselves of,

A – This note has been lost. How could it be reconstructed? It cannot. It is bootless as the effort to determine the time through reference to a stopped or broken watch. "Surely," one thinks, "knowing, as we do, the time the watch stopped must have some worth, all I need do is to determine the interval since then, and I shall know the current time."

In which we see, yet again, the human capacity for self-delusion. For the fact that the watch was constructed to tell the and does the mind not function, in the main, however we might wish to think it otherwise, to the detriment, to the *undoing* of the body?

O, better, then, Sport, I say, than Philosophy, for the getting of "Wisdom" – for there is no Wisdom. There is only Folly; and any fool could see they were two different dogs.

time bespeaks no hidden or residuary excellencies on its part once that operation's ceased.

Now, like the corpse of man, it now exists only to call our attention to the absence of that which we once had ta'en for granted. No. No, like the corpse, it can tell us nothing now save the fact it once could tell us something.[A1*]

1 – "How dead the dead look. With good reason." Greind. Cf. his *Thoughts on a Cessation of Being*, from chapter 12:

I was once in church. And the pastor's sermon concluded with the phrase from scripture, "Let the dead bury the dead," at which utterance I heard, at my side, a feminine voice mutter, "Who's stopping them?" and I turned my head to glimpse, for the first time, the young woman who'd, one day, become my first wife.

* What of the operations of pathology? How can one take this otherwise than as an intentional slight?

Jane of Trent

Jane of Trent

But who *was* Jane of Trent?

Can it be established that she/it ever existed?

"Sant'Graal/Sang Real" was the cry of an earlier age.

Imagine those adventure-loving stalwarts of that time – mounting their horses or mules and trotting off "around the world" – their mission: to discover that object whose very existence was in doubt, and whose identity, to compound the difficulty, unknown.[1]

Some said it was a cup (*grandalis*), and some a grating (*gratilis*).

Some, looking for new fish to fry, elaborated the first into Chalice, Basin, Bowl, *et cetera*; the second to Casket, Box . . .

(Is it not interesting that the one stress the circular, spherical, or demi-spherical; the other the square or cubic?

It has been noted that the world's religious symbols each portray the play of opposites: the vertical-and-horizontal of the cross, the opposed triangles of the shield of David, two wacky half-circles of the Yin and Yang, the pierced planet of the Crypto-Janissaries, etc., etc. – and might we not deduce, infer or extrapolate a greater, say, an *ur*-bipolarity in the voyages and efforts of the Crusaders after the Grail? Might we not say they strove not to (or primarily to) possess an object, but to codify a symbol? Or, to put it differently, to ally their name to such codification – for, had they obtained that Grail (whatever the deuce it may have been) they surely would have been forced (a) to surrender it to ecclesiastic authority, and (b) at some point, to die.

What would remain? Some measure of fame.[2] So what?

Similarly the quest to identify, to isolate, to establish the existence of Jane of Trent smacks of the neurotic's (hero's) task: to unify

1 – See Walter Wade, B.A., *It Could Have Been a Toaster.*

2 – Cf. *You Only Rent It* (etc.)

opposites, to discover the Hid, to discard the false, and, so, still anomie.)

Who, what, was Jane of Trent?

Let us proceed analytically.

(1) What was Trent?

I will now take the reader through what is, I hope, more than an approximation of my mental processes; or, if you will, of my use in approaching similar conundrums.

I cannot say, and I will not call it a "technique" – it may or may not be – I think I may apply the more non-value-laden term, "procedure."

It has long been my use to sequester myself when facing a (seemingly) difficult problem, thus to allow my unconscious to work.

Having no discipline, I find that the least distraction is seized upon and exploited past any rational forecast of its inherent interest or utility. I would, for example, pick up an old ticket stub and study it, in the absence of anything else.

I would read the manufacturer's warning upon the venetian blinds, the upholstery tag which says DO NOT REMOVE THIS TAG, film reviews, South American literature, *any*thing, in short, in preference to the hard (but so oft rewarding) work of the Imagination.

There I sit, then, in that which I've come to think of as "seclusion" – in my old, cracked, brown and comfortable wing chair, my feet in the carpet slippers, my shoulders draped in the old, moth-holed cardigan (what is there so comforting about old clothes?) – the pipe and its appurtenances on the smoking stand, the case bottle of sherry on the sideboard, shades half-drawn, the window cracked, my old ink-spattered writing board across my lap. In the appointed depression on its top the Schaeffer™ snorkel pen, filled and wiped. Upon the board, flush to its left-hand margin, several (more than ten but rarely more than twenty) sheets of laid, ivory, A4 (or "foolscap") paper.

(. . . how I miss Monica – the finest bitch that ever was.

And yet, how privileged I was to've known her.

What God, what deranged Deity would doom these creatures, their lives so short, so cruelly short, in any case, to displasia.

Were I a billionaire I would devote all of my resources to eradication of this scourge.

I know that in this I am not alone. I praise the work of Mrs. Truesdale and of the Society – their work is beyond praise.

But even their support must leave a gap between the memory of that Bright Friendship, of those morning walks, of the exchange of glances that, yes, can only be called "private jokes," of the sighs which could only be "confidences," and the reality of this dreary, empty, interminable loneliness.

"Woof woof" – how to convey the tone, the *tones*, more to the point, which indicated *Here I am*; *I'm hungry*; *What is that?*; *I'm glad to see you*; *Something is amiss*, and all degrees beyond and between, of speech, of perception, reason, intuition, of a grasp of the world so far beyond mine . . .

How can I exorcize the spectre of her limping, in pain, eyes full not of that "mute questioning," which the unperceptive or (frankly) exploitative would foist upon us in the name of sentiment, no, but, to the contrary, of a full perception – full knowledge, full realization of her impending doom. "They are better off, for they do not know their end," spout the uneducated.

What a load of crap.

I wish they would have been there when I put her down.

I wish they could have . . . but I digress.)

Now I am "set": my artefacts, my tools, my "friends" (or, say, so as not to fall into sententiousness, "comforters") are all about me – the door is locked, the telephone is "off the hook," I can begin . . .

If only Monica were here . . .

[End.]

The paper was graded B, the grade scrawled across the title sheet in red. Under it, the assessment, "Too sad."

On the second page, again in red, at the top, "*Margins . . . ???*"

From Self Help and Purity for Girls

For, of course the Universe was, at its largest, discovered to be not only congruent, but identical to the smallest previously unsuspected particle of matter, this being the beloved circularity which was the last refuge of the frustrated physicist attempting to describe the infinity of Space.

And all the science-fiction writers had been right. How *jolly*. And all he could think was of the unfortunate, the pathetic impossibility of a man on the largest and a woman on the smallest world having a sexual encounter.

"Which goes to show you," his wife said.

But it was not for nothing he was Chief of the Institute. Not for nothing at all.

How well, in fact, he had improved the hours of "leisure," the supposed "lunch" hours during his long years of employment there.

How he had benefited from their trust, or, say, their lack of systematic inventory oversight.

For, now, it stood before him: THE MACHINE . . . assembled in lieu of – how many? – chicken-salad sandwiches. THE MACHINE.

Who would not have said that its construction was a pipe dream?

Nay, a symptom of obsession so deep as to deserve its own cognomen – its own specie of awe or revulsion?

"It's a good thing I didn't tell anybody!" he thought, as he looked upon it.

"What adventure awaits me!" he thought.

He shed his shoes and stepped upon the platform.

He threw the preliminary switches in their long-ago pre-ordained order. What was *that*, however?

Someone rattling the maintenance supply area door . . .

He looked back. He heard their voices.

Why, *at this one time*, he wondered – why this, of all times . . .?

Any residual scruple, and, yes, any fear was discarded.

This was his one chance. He depressed the final buttons in the precise-numbered sequence. The board began to glow, the platform to vibrate, awaiting the final activation.

He grasped the lever. They were breaking down the door. But they were too late! The lever was on its way down. He smiled. He looked down at his feet upon the platform – those feet which would carry him on an adventure the like of which was never known before. And he saw, on the platform, sharing the platform with him, a carpenter ant. A carpenter ant, crawling, now, upon his naked foot, as the force field enveloped him, and all went bright, then dark, then bright for the longest time, after which there was nothing.

"Where am I?" he thought upon awakening. *Et cetera.*

Sensing, one might say, were one to go that way
From *Trentiana* – Elders of the Order, "Sleigh Bells" issue, December 2320.

Sensing, one might say, were one to go that way, feeling the scend (or "send") of the time-to-come, or, say, the "future" (as which of us, time-to-time, has not; though we may well deny it. But what does it profit us, to turn our back upon that knowledge, like the Comstock People, striving to block access to sexual information. Or, as if . . . but I digress.)

Sensing, the scend of the future, then, like a salt mariner, astride the deck of his life, if I may, sensing, finally, or call it perception, if you will, for who can know, to call it premonition or delusion? Only that person for whom it had come true.

[Here occurs, and is omitted, a diversion occasioned by a troop of motorcycle paparazzi. The couple in question had stolen out of a restaurant for a love tryst, and thought themselves well away. But had discovered their pursuers close behind, and bidding fair to follow come "hell" or "high water."

The two celebrated lovers sped off in their car, increasing their speed as if such would increase their chance of privacy. The driver–bodyguard looked back to assess his progress and plowed the car into a stone abutment.

And many have thought of Actaeon, turned into a stag, pursued by his own hounds. But none mentioned the little mother and her child, upon which the limousine bore down at the beginning of the chase. How different, then, that morrow's news, and how, it would have been seen that ignominy was their fell, unavoidable fate, how one would have discerned its lineaments then, in the couple's very act.

That dénouement of the play for which they had been born, and that appalling lesson the apotheosis of the entertainment that their lives has been. For which of us is better than those bow-tied astrologers, the economists, who teach us every morning why the stock or bond market has done this or that, but are and remain impotent to prognosticate it?]

"No, what is cause and what effect?" the Old Man said; "and, more to the point, how is it that we are continually gulled by these post-facto pseudo-prognosticators, these false sages, past-posting us and calling it prescience?" Here he paused, and sighed, "Or 'common sense'? I hate them all," he said, "and wish they were all boiled in oil. Or locked in a walk-in freezer with nothing to read.

"However," he continued, "be it a clairvoyant vision, or be it that fantasy of greatness grown from our own egoism – whichever, in the end, Lincoln possessed, or possessed him – how can we say, and how is one to parse that which may have been delusion but which was borne out by subsequent events?"

This was the phenomenologic question: Can that demonstrated to have been foretold be dismissed, after the foretold event, as coincidence? This was the question which occupied Wilson sufficiently to have included it eleven counted times in diaries dating from his adolescence through the White House years – the next-to-last in that pathetic scrawl, the last in the feminine hand proved to've been his wife's – supposedly dictated, generally assumed to've been her own invention; but how, finally, is one to say, for are not the semanticist, the philologic detective, the graphologist, merely the modern rendition of the paid co-respondent? I think so.

"Lincoln walked five miles to school."

How that must have impressed itself upon the adolescent mind, for which of us, in that age, does not long, *yearn* for, insist upon a model? What engines of self-sacrifice and idealism are the young! How struck by the commonplace, co-opted by the false, and blind to the oh-so-slightly hidden, workings of the world – how manipulable, how sad, how dear . . .

[The manuscript here is spattered with what was thought for a time to be tears, but which color reproduction seemed to reveal as blood, and which was proved by a spectrographic analysis to be beet and potato soup, the base being, interestingly, neither chicken nor beef, but *goose*!!!]

. . . that Lincoln walked (he continued) five miles to school each day, that it was taken as a prescience on his part, for why would he have troubled, absent his (quite correct) valuation of its worth in advertising, in light of the fact that the school was right across the street? To quote from his diaries:*

. . . rose every day at dawn to circle his own house for that hour-and-a-half thought sufficient to have walked five miles. And then regained his house, consumed the breakfast his "ma" had set out, picked up his books and stepped across the street. *Ding dong*, the bell must have went. And we may share his dilemma, those mornings when he'd risen late: "What to do . . .? What to do . . .?"

The phrase rang in Monica's head – "What to do?" – as the waiter returned with the tea. He saw her consternation. She looked up.

"You *did* say 'India,' miss? Or 'Ceylon'?"

"I said 'coffee'," she said. "Could you then tell me, in the name of everything good, how you could possibly have come to understand it as 'tea'?"

The phrase from Hazlitt – so useful so oft – returned to her mind: "The truest test of superiority is never to be upset by impertinence."

At which precise moment the doors blew in, and there was Mikey, in the long fur coat – that same fur coat she'd seen over the back of the chaise-longue in Sloane Square, the ice crystals still upon the collar, as her head turned to the side, his breath in her ear. "Yes. Yes. Yes. Yes," and so on, and she wondered, not for the first, no, nor for the twentieth time, why she could never retain the definition of the term "guard hairs."

---

* Wilson's.

The Lake Poets can kiss my ass

or: *My ducts, my daughter*, by a Member of the Medical Profession; this being, of course, that interrogatory eventually replaced by "The Sample Paragraph",[1] see p. 81.

"What is an electrical impulse?" These are the words which greeted Tom Burns on his first day in Professor Hodgkin's class. They appeared at the head of chapter 12, not in the Professor's (assigned) *Etiology of Behavior*, but in a sweat-stained paperback edition of *Expo Summer*.

"What is this trash doing on my desk?" Tom was surprised to find he'd spoken aloud. His query was answered by a throaty chuckle, and Tom turned to see a burly, bluff, good-natured-looking chap beside him.

"Thought I'd catch up on some lighter reading," the fellow said. "Sorry if it puts you out. Seems we're going to be sharing this desk; that being so, guess we'd better 'howdy-and-shake': I'm Butch Palmer," and he held out a hand which proved to be warm, dry, and friendly when Tom took it in his own.

> List the *major* themes introduced in the above paragraphs. Having listed them, rest, if rest can come to you in this vale of tears. Rest and reflect upon whatever subject, mood, or memory suggests itself to you. Remembering always to breathe through the nose, the breath flowing back against the rear of the throat such that it produces a slight "rasp" or roughness. Follow the breath down, down, drawing it down through the stomach, down, as if one pivoted the hips backward, the breath following, down to the anus, held, held, held, and, then released. So slowly. Slower, slower still; for what is breath but life? It goes, but to return; it returns but to reissue, again, and in again, the paradigm of all life, the essence of life, getting and spending, learning, and forgetting.*

1 – See *Two Trains Are Leaving Chicago*, op. cit.

---

* "Kissing and telling" [*disputed*].

What can the point of any of it be? There can be no point to it, no, not even meditation on some, or upon its absence. "*It*" is all it is. That's it. Breathe in, breathe out. That's all it ever was. The rest is advertising: man and woman, Chet and Donna, dog and cat, B and D, any and all, false and, yes, finally arbitrary oppositions, syn-, hom-, antonyms, identities, that parlor game we come to call philosophy, that whistling-in-the-dark.

"Yes, but," the Jester said, "what about closing time, when all the girls look prettier, and the night is so long?"

"Well, that's a different story," the Old Wrangler said.

"Please, then, address it," Jester beseeched.

"I will speak of closing time," the Wrangler said, and sighed, "upon the understanding that I mean it to mean neither more, no, nor less, than that time at which they call 'Last call,' an' 'You don't have to go home, but you can't stay here,'" and he began:

"There I was, the beer gone flat. Salt could not bring it back. The purple-pink stirrers were looped into themselves, which offered, to the drunk and sober mind, a vista of innumerable possibilities, but which, in the event, could but be worked into some variation of a neater or less-neat circle, square, figure-of-eight, or other closed system. It had been straight, now it was closed, and we then move on to another. Not unlike our progress to the next drink, cigarette, love, compulsive action, thought, addiction, meal, breath . . ."

Here the attendants arrived, and took, one on each arm, the Old Wrangler back to his room.

Jester sighed, and picked up his book.

"Where the Wattage is unknown, and our investigation is shifted, necessarily, to the Resistance," he read.

"No," he thought, "it is sufficient. It is not the life I would have chosen, had I had the choice, but it is a good life."

An Adumbration of the Inner Code

Where the inner code is treated as if it existed; for, how else, were one so inclined, to understand in order to dismiss it?

"No, no, no, no," she said, "but they are knocking at my door."

The once supposed lifeless form of her husband stared on, eyes directed to the fourth rose down the left of the William Morris wallpaper they had planned (together) to employ to enliven the room.

"But yet he breathes," she thought, "and that must be my consolation. Who will care for him, however, when I am taken away. And, equally, who will Care for the Country?"

Thwack. Thwack. Thwack.

"They are resorting to hammers," she thought, "hammers or mauls, for I never have been able to keep the two sufficiently separated in my mind . . ."

She recurred to an autumn morning, in New Hampshire, at the farm.

Her husband, still youthful and powerful, though fifty, swinging that above his head which was either a hammer or a maul, and she looking on, proudly, her pride not untouched by that never totally absent anxiety for his health.

"Woodrow," she'd said, "we must consider your *health*."

"Nothing better for it," he'd retorted. "Good for the pecs, the abs, the lats, the bis and triceps. Very little which it won't improve. Best exercise there is, swinging a twelve-pound . . ."

And here the recollection dissolved, the word was lost as she saw, for the thousandth, nay, the millionth time, the scene dissolve, or, better, contract to the vision of his prissy mouth, spewing blood, as he fell over the chopping block, the maul or hammer dropping to his side, while someone's voice screamed, "Corpsman!"

And now here she was, *no* one to help her, no one left to intercede, as the door splintered, and the Men in the White Coats approached, so carefully.

"Now, Ginger," the fat one said, "now, *Ginger*, it's time for our shot."

He passed between her and the television, and, as was her wont, she spat.

She felt his arms pinioning her, and made as if to submit, relaxing her body for a moment. Then the needle found her vein, and she had no more need to feign lassitude. Nor had she the power, as she spiraled downard. Her last thought a frantic "But the *President* . . . the League of *Nations* . . ."

End of the Second Section

The Fox knows many things.
The Etrog knows One Big Thing.
AESOP, *THE WIND IN THE WILLOWS*

Then farewell to Jane of Trent – farewell, Jane, and farewell to Bennigsen, and to the intrigues of the Swedish crown, and to the self-effacing Scandinavian beloved of literature.

Where did we ever see an evil Swede?*

Farewell to battles, farewell to swords, farewell to medals and ribbons of gold and blue, farewell to fresh, thick butter from the churn, to white nights by the ——,[1] mornings without fatigue, the day both introduced and softened by that rich, fine butter to which the *drapiers* must have alluded in the Scandinavian flags.

Oh, Bennigsen – how cold your grave, how undeserved your end – how much more fitting to the hero tale had you lived to embrace the Princess. You are bathed† not by the reverent, and not by the seasonable, loving tears of clean, filial sentiment, no, but by the lacrimations of the maudlin, of that unwashed and less-than-lettered readership[2] to whom you are but a convenient fiction. O irony! No wonder that the poets live in your thrall – thou Greater-than-the-Gods.[3]

Now all that rises must converge, the non-Euclideans exclaim. Must not their observation (of geometry) hold equally true of the Ironic, by the operations of which high and low, fear and pity, surprise and foreknowledge, all, in short, are‡ (re?)united.

What of Jane of Trent?

1 – (River T.K.).
2 – Of *Bongazine.*
3 – With all apologies to any religious readers. The author is supposed, and the editors avow the lack of any intent to insult or transgress the usually agreed upon *moeurs* of polite discourse. Within which bounds they hope all reasonable readers will find this disclaimer to lie.

* Death Larsen, the "Sea Wolf." † Figuratively. ‡ Is?

Section Three

As "God" is trifurcated into three essences, which are, then, played against four into that eternal dodecanensis of the seasons, disciples, Tribes of Israel, steps to partial sobriety, and, then, reformulated into its essentials – four becoming two in the hope that three, eventually, will become one.

MUUGUU

The Boathouse

Chet and Donna

In which it is suggested a previous chief executive wrote a celebrated address on the lack of an elephant.

I make bold to quote from the (pencil) manuscript, the *first* draft of *Newport Summer*, to the "short story", "Chet and Donna in the Boathouse." Chet is speaking:

"You know, Donna," he said, as he brushed the sand off of his elbows, "you know, I don't think the Professor is that far off base."

"But, Chet," she said, "I don't understand. Why would he write about the *lack* of an elephant?"

He smiled. "Honey," he said. He shook his head. No, now *could* she understand? Her knowledge of war was limited to those daguerreotypes in Grandfather's rolltop. What could she know of "The Platoon in the Attack", or "Kill or Get Killed: The Infantryman's Guide to Sentry Elimination", to *any* of it, in short?

"Honey," he said, "to understand you have to look at the respective positions of the Union and the Confederacy at the time of the Address, and to one engine of warfare, shunned for centuries and never seen on this continent, an engine, however, perfectly suited – his advisers said – to combat in the coastal plain, in that area which the Ironclads denied to Yankee shipping: the pachyderm."

Her eyes grew soft with love. "He's just so *smart*," she thought.

Alligators
Deleted from the "Chet" section of *Rybecki's Dream*

He had been told when he was young that alligators sleep on top of each other stacked like cordwood.

It (the phrase) had informed his life, and had, in fact, become his life – both the pursuit and the paradigm of pursuit, of his waking hours – the attempt at verification of the proposition.

On meeting an attractive woman, for example, he would think to himself,* "Yes, she seems a 'real good sort.' However, how would one, finally, 'know', not having seen her, at night, in the deep, under water, stacked up with her kind . . ." *et cetera.*

How he both shone and sparkled in the first half-hours, for example, of the first party or gathering in any new group of acquaintance! And then there appeared, as his friends oft described it, "that look."

And, "No. No, not *this* time!" he thought. "Not this time."

"I've so enjoyed myself," he said.

"I have, too," [she said] said the young lady.[1] "Well . . ." she said. "Well . . ."

"You have to go back to work?" he said.

"Actually, *no*," she said. "It's a half-holiday . . ."

The invitation was clear, and, emboldened, he responded to it.

"Perhaps a *walk*?" he suggested.

"Oh, excellent," Ginger said. "Or, we could, we could go to the *zoo . . .!*"

"No. *No*," he thought. "NO!"

She looked at him. "Anything the *matter*?" she asked.

"*No, not* the zoo," he said. "NOT . . ."

And he thought, "Well, I guess that this is why they call it an *obsession*."

1 – "said Ginger" (var. edn).

* How could he think otherwise?

"Well," she said, "what about the planetarium . . .?"

And that is how he (a) contracted herpes; and (b) ended up on Mars.

Is this story an example of *bathos* or *pathos*?[2]

2 – "or d'Artagnan"; this scrawled in the margins of a "reading copy" in the Carnegie Library, New South Mars – "Where your friends are."

From Newport Summer

Let us examine the inscription on the boathouse door:

Those who write on bathroom walls
Should roll their shit in little balls
And those who read what they have writ
Should eat those little balls of shit.[1]

It was given to me to have been one of the group which discovered the original manuscript, in the poolroom, where it corrected the roll of a 5 × 10 Brunswick, Balke-Collender, Monarch (*c.* 1843).

I prize, as do we all, the round impressions, page by page, made by that table's foot.

I do not, as some do, however, construe the words and sentences so capsulated into an infra-, nay, an *ur*-, if you will, composition.

In so doing one posits, of course, a super-intelligence. One both creates and ascribes to a new religion.

But of this why not not of that?

Why not of *any* random realignment of intelligence? And must we not all, finally, consider it a worship of *un*reason to say, "all meaning resides in everything"?[2]

May we not torture any proposition into uselessness? May we not proclaim pure scholarship resembles nothing so much as the rubber band – its *sine qua non*, elasticity, an invitation to disaster?

1 – Bautz et al. (eds), *There Stands a Woman with Soap in her Hole* (2011).
2 – "See the World in a Grain on Sand", *Business Opportunities in Egypt and the Holy Land* (USIA pamphlet, ?1930).

Dink Stover at Yale

A fragment, believed to be from Aristotle, *Dink Stover at Yale*[1]

Yale, long the festering breeding ground of that country's Intelligence Services, the dark secret, the Clan which dare not speak its name, that conclave not unlike and, in fact, balancing on the Right its opposite number, Bohemia, wherein Scotch and adultery stood in for mind drugs and free love, and the postulants went out not to seduce to sexual and aesthetic latitude and self-absorption but to banana wars across the world, cozy and warm in the hierarchic self-satisfied – we will not say "certainty," for, finally, their creed was not more outward-directed than that of the Beatnik; the one operating under the Ensign Art, the other Polity, but each more than content to revel in the communitarily awarded perquisites, for which they were prepared to kill or die, the one from overdose, from sexual disease, the other at the head of a suborned column of supposed insurgents, marching – but I warp my metaphor in over-extension and it sags like the catenary.[2] "When will I learn, O Lord, who maketh both the East and West, and sends down the White Race, to ravage the Land till its stink in the nostrils makes one long for Death? I wonder if the eggs are done . . ."

1 – Imitation being the sincerest form of plagiarism: "Two sperms looking at an egg. One says to the other, 'Makes me wish I was born.'" (Twelfth Vatican Council on Birth Control, Intercourse, Pa., 20??).[A]

2 – N.B. Stateville Prison, Joliet, Ill., 19??: "Richard Loeb, youngest student ever to graduate from the University of Chicago, last night ended his sentence with a proposition."

A – Note used by permission. I cite also: *The Perry Como Sweater, Its Provenance*; *Jump Back: The Life of Lord Cardigan*, and *Cloak of My Colors* [?*Cork of Many Colors*]: *Racial Diversity in Cork and Kerry*, *Irish Echo* (Sunday Supplement and Classified [date?]); and the MIT Publications monograph, submitted in partial fulfilment of the requirements for a degree, Doctor of Philosophy in Earth Science, *Toward a Real Number Parameter on the Ways to Skin a Cat*, and its film version, *Let Common Sense Prevail* (or, in S. American release, *Skippy*).

Philology
Source: *Newport Summer*

www.chetndonna.boathouse.com (in random search, by *frequency*, *word association*, and *philologic average*[1]) yielded:

1 Ginger
2 Real property
3 Incarceration: *Ginger Sees Chet and Donna at the "Old Wilson Place"* (original title: *Trapped*)

"Who *is* that cunt, Chet?" Donna said, her long legs thrown carelessly over his hard, sun-browned stomach.

They heard the sweet tenor throbbing of the *Chriscraft* as it made its way down the cove – such a fine, old-fashioned sound.

". . . who *is* she, fir chrissake?"

But Chet was asleep. Lulled by the sun, the sex, the rhythm of the day, two hookers of fine, pale Amontillado sherry, filched from the butler's pantry at the Lodge, and 4 ccs of intravenous synthetic morphine (Chacranovid) in the big vein behind the knee.

"Ah, shit," Donna thought. "Ah, shit. I'll have to lug the damn picnic basket up the hill myself, and I'll get chafed on my shins from the wicker bouncing against me the whole time. Why can't they design those things so's they'll be easier to *carry* . . .?"

Then the door blew open. Donna looked up to see a young woman with a gun. Looming above her was the Aggrieved Paramour, Vengeance, a Woman Scorned: the answer to her question, and the answer was: That cunt was Ginger. *Blam blam blam blam blam*. The bullets rocked her body.

"Gulp," she thought. "They'll hear *that* up at the old Wilson place . . .!"

1 – According to generally accepted standards of accepting, Lutz, Frost, et al., *Questions and Answers in Bookkeeping*.

And then she was dead.

Chet floated past her, in the guise of a fish, as did her father, then several containers which she understood as holding Weetabix. Then she was standing before a white-coated tribunal.

"If this isn't the beatingest thing I ever did see," she thought. "I will eat my hat."

She longed, she burned for the presence of a comrade – someone with whom to share this final irony: that death was quite precisely as pictured in those works she'd always judged empty both of talent and imagination.

"This is one for the books," she thought, and then the Judge of the Tribunal spoke.

"What do you get," he said, "if you cross a chicken and an Irish terrier?"

". . . *huh*," she thought.

Donna looked down and realized she was floating. Above the world.

But the world above which she floated was not geography, but Time.

". . . all right, then," she thought.

Most instructive, looking down, were those incidents she had forgotten.

Incidents which, at the time, seemed crucial, essential, formative, tragic, life-changing, and which she'd discarded or repressed.

"Oh, my gosh," she thought, "there I am in the closet with Mom's masseur . . ."

There was a rustling of wings.

A big bird took her in its claws and swam through the air to a mountain eerie, where it dropped her into a large nest.

Two warring notions clashed in her mind: (a) this is comfy; and (b) what the fuck is going on?

In *Trapped*, the scene here shifts to Ginger in prison, formulating her last words:

"I'm not afraid of you sonsabitches, cause you can't do anything to me worse than the stuff I've done to you . . ."

"Naa, fuck it," she thought. "Why give them the satisfaction?"

She turned her attention to her "last meal": chipped beef on toast, stuffed cabbage, and "junket."

"*I'll* show 'em who's tough," she thought. "*I'll* show 'em who's tough. I'll *eat* it!"

But Chet was dead. He was dead, that hunk. Never again would he stride, "young, dumb, and full of come," into the "Beef Encounter." Never would he . . . *et cetera*.

We skip to chapter 12:

"But *wait* a second," Donna thought. "Hold *on*, here . . ." She took a deep breath. "*This* isn't Heaven . . . This is *Mars*!"

Here follows the disquisition on the history and purpose of capital punishment.

The Trial of Ginger

The insanity defense examined. In which the defenders argue their principal acted from a lack of reason, and the State's representative that the crime was sane.

PROSECUTOR: . . . you thought you were Mrs. Wilson . . .?

GINGER: The first or the second?

PROSECUTOR: I beg your pardon?

(*Conference at the state's table.*)

Yes. The second.

GINGER: No.

PROSECUTOR: You thought you were the *first*?

GINGER: No.

(*Conference at the state's table.*)

PROSECUTOR: Then why did you ask "the first or the second?"

(*Long pause.*)

(*To Judge Motts*) May I approach the bench?

(*Counsel approach the bench. Conference at the bench. Mumble mumble mumble. Counsel return.*)

How are you feeling today, Ginger?

(*Pause. Defendant weeps. Pause.*)

JUDGE: . . . may I suggest . . .

GINGER: I'm fine. I'm fine.

JUDGE: . . . if you would like . . .

GINGER: I'm fine.

JUDGE: . . . may I finish, please?

(*Pause. The Judge arranges papers on his desk. The weeping stops.*)

I was going to say: if you feel you would benefit from a short recess, this court would . . .

(*Weeping begins again.*)

DEFENSE COUNSEL: . . . Your Honor . . .

JUDGE: . . . if you cannot control your client, I shall hold you in contempt.

DEFENSE COUNSEL: Your Honor . . .

JUDGE: . . . yes.

DEFENSE COUNSEL: Your Honor, if it please the court . . .

JUDGE: I *am* the court. (*Pause.*) I *am* the court. You don't have to say "Your Honor" and, "May it please the court." I *am* the court. (*Pause.*) It's as if you said, "Your Honor, may it please Your Honor . . ." (*Pause.*) It's obsequious.

DEFENSE COUNSEL: Beg the court's pardon.

JUDGE: Proceed.

DEFENSE COUNSEL: Your Honor . . .

JUDGE: . . . yes.

DEFENSE COUNSEL: (*Consults notes.*) Who can compel the human heart . . . ?[1]

From the Opinion

. . . when will man's nature be comprehensible? This will occur when Hell freezes over and all the little devils go ice-skating.[2]

1 – The remainder of this speech has – mercifully, as we may opine – been lost.
2 – He means, of course, that the *likelihood* of it occurring is *as* the likelihood of the aforementioned winter (or "Alpine") sports. A computation made more difficult* by the fantastical or notional nature of the second term.[A]

A – One tradition holds that the sentence or *bon mot* ends, ". . . in their picturesque Scandinavian knitwear."†

* Impossible! Impossible! † Would that we lived in a world where such could, unquestioned, be accepted as the case.

Stuffed in the Airlock

Those sheets which "kept the life in the Capsule until Help arrived." Here presented, traditionally, in the order in which they were extracted.

The Petition
or: "The First Sheet"

The problem is this – or, to put it differently, "This is the problem" – I am "reluctant," as the Gardener said, to put my name on anything which would – and you know that I am – disturb the status "quo." I do not know the facts of the case sufficiently to offer an opinion other than: "It looks like many and right-thinking people are het up on both sides of the issue." But this sentiment, although "formally" acceptable and fine and so on, fills me, as I rehearse uttering it, with a sense of incompletion and self-loathing.

So now is the time, I think, to consider, no, not the issue "*per se*" but that *mechanism* whereby we decide "that there must be two sides to the story," and, having so decided, set out to create them.

Because, hell, *are* there, *must* there be "two sides"? I don't think so, for:

1 I think that this dictum *itself* is a perfect example of one-sidedness, as we're just meant to eat it, *ex cathedra*, and
2 all this froofraw about "evenhandedness" is just a bunch of crap put out there by those who gain *not* by peace, synthesis, rest, relaxation, no, but *by* there existing conflict: teachers, cops, editors, you know . . .

Or, or, that, perhaps, there might *be* "two sides," but who is it that *says* it?

All the people on the other side.

For, if not, it's just, "Let me talk myself out of the things I've thought, because I'm No Damn Good, and my parents are right," or somesuch.

And now you ask me to sign up with you. To "throw my hat in the ring," and to endorse *what very well may be* a position which, *had I thought of it*, I could support with no trouble at all. *But.* To be asked to enlist in the aid of one of which I must think – as you're asking me to sign a petition *against* it – has to be a *conflict*, in which two positions exist; and, to add salt to the wound, to do it without even having time to "weigh" both sides; and *plus* which, which is, to me, the unfortunate, the *artificial thing*: to get caught in that immemorial trick bag of "There are two sides: choose one," and in all *that* arbitrariness – this is a situation I had hoped my age and so forth would excuse me from.

But he who flies from strife just trades the one thing for the other. And here I am *lathering* myself, in an attempt to escape conflict! How funny.

Now to the merits of the case. I understand them incompletely.

But, if I *did* understand them, or with a *gun* to my head, I'd have to side, *not* with, as you have named it, "free thought," no, but with the *Institute.*

Forgive me, if you must, but, surely (I think) that is what one harvests if one sows discord.

Call me a Communist, that's what I think.

Further, I think that petitions are just a load of crap.

Who reads them, except people who thought that way in *any* case.

Or their opponents – just to indulge in a(n) "orgy of indignation?"

Power comes from the end of a gun.

Save your breath.

BOBBY

Tom Tiddler's Fancy
or: *Why Do Mice Like Cheese?*
"The Second Sheet"

Oh Jimmy Twiddlemouse was a chipper and happy fellow that spring day.

Had his mother not fitted him out in quite the cunningest yellow knee britches and his favorite let-down flannel tartan shirt? Indeed she had. And now he fairly bursted with pride as he skipped down the lane.

"Where are you off to, rushing so lively, then?" said Ellen, the Stoat.

"I will tell you," Jimmy Twiddlemouse replied. "But you must promise not to tell."

"Cross my heart and hope to die," squealed Ellen. "Should I prove false to my vow, may all the tortures of the Inquisition befall me. Including but not limited to: beheading, disembowelling, stones, hot oil, the rack, the pit, the iron maiden . . ."

This was a new side to his friend, and Jimmy stood by amazed whilst she continued.

". . . the oubliette, the bastinado; torture or removal of eyes, fingers, genitals . . ."

He was impressed both by her choice of diversion, and by her obvious commitment to it, and her scholarship therein, bespeaking an extraordinary application.

"I had no *idea*," he thought, "that she was capable of such *address* . . ."

". . . the scree, the net, the 'Wife of Bath', the fish ladder, any and all, one or severally, administered in any order, combination or derivative." With which she spit on her palm, and crossed it, *per saltire*, over that place she presumed most approximating the position of the heart.[1]

1 – The true position of the heart, in all mammals, lies almost precisely upon the

meridian, and not, as is erroneously supposed, slightly to the left.[A]

A – There appears to be a direct correlation between the education of the individual and the individual's disposition to minimize the distance between the position of the heart and the body's center line – the uneducated picturing it lying below the left nipple, the intellectual *just* to the left of center. All are, of course, wrong, but it must be observed that the less educated, though guilty of the greater error geographically, are decreasingly (as their misconception deviates from the center line) guilty of intellectual arrogance.

When All Is Said and Done
"The Third Sheet" or "Wrapper"

"People say, 'when all is said and done,' *but who demands it?*" Ginger screamed, and lapsed back into her dream of the Red Planet – into her dream of Mars.

". . . in that fugue motif which," Dr Friedman said, "must have accomplished *something* positive, as she did it so *often*."

"But," replied Dr. Mott, "yes, but, why would we assume that it was *helpful*? Shouldn't we, to the contrary, assume it was other-than-helpful?" He paused. "Isn't that the definition of *disease*?"

They glowered at each other across the conference table, with an enmity both unclothed and unlimited.

Meanwhile, Ginger writhed on the floor.

"Woof woof woof woof," she barked, striving to still the tumult she perceived around her.

The two medics rolled on the floor, fighting as men fight who are neither schooled nor disposed to it, in the hope some technique or some mechanism will emerge spontaneously, grown through their rage, to grant them the victory; and wrath, increasingly, at themselves for their previously unsuspected, their new-discovered and traitorous inabilities – each discovering quickly that age-old and most practical of maxims: "Kick him in the balls."

Ginger continued in her dream of Mars.

"Mars is far away," she said to herself. "And I think of it in that voice which must be My Own, as it is so familiar. And I recognize it. But I only hear it in my head, I hear it when I read, and I hear it when I *think* of things. I hear it now saying that I hear it now, and saying that my thoughts and the Voice are the same thing."

"Mars Mars Mars Mars Mars," the dream went on. "This is my dream of Mars."

"Chet are Donna are one" – here the book ends.[1]

1 – Chet and Donna are two, as two they are one; and Ginger is one, which is, of course, three,[A] which, once again makes one. So it has always been found "nice" that their narrative "completes" the disquisition.[B]

A – $\begin{array}{r} 2 \\ +1 \\ \hline 3 \end{array}$

B – Which was written, and was understood to mean, "that portion prior to 'The Old Wrangler'."

Esquimaux
An interpolation

> That it was happening in fact did not and could not indicate that it was, in fact, not happening, coincidentally, in fantasy – that megalomaniacal dream, of fame, of success, wealth and adulation – and did not make it any the less emotionally and psychologically pernicious.
>
> PEDRO KHAN, *BENNIGSEN: A LIFE*

From Greind's Journal:

Cf. "Eskimo pussy is mighty cold"[1] by the Institute for Northern Studies, Edmonton, Alberta.

QUESTION: What was the *third* influence upon Shelley?

Any link, at this remove, must, of course, be suppository.

Let us, however, pick up a "worn-out tool" (Kipling, "If").

The tool to which I refer is that of Deconstructionism.

But a deconstruction is based *not* upon statistical analysis, neither that "reduction" (for a fuller discussion of "reduction," kiss my arse), but, rather, that based not unlike that elephant beloved of the ancients on whose back rested the world, and who, himself, stood four-square on the back of a giant* turtle, based, *based* I say, upon something *firm and unmoving*: upon *randomness*. Upon *chaos*, upon a criminal, nay, a psychotic aversion to meaning. Let us deconstruct (restructure) the sentence thus:

Cold, pretty Eskimo is pussy.

What have we learned?

1 – Cf. Alcock and (?)Brown, *Brittle Women*: "I don't know, but I been told, Eskimo pussy . . ." *et cetera*.

---

* *Vast*, actually.

That someone (the implied or supposed speaker, averrer, holder of opinion) finds an Eskimo "pretty."[2]

It would, of course, be remarkable[3] were the Eskimo *not* cold.

And, so, we skip on to the thrust, the burden of the deconstructed piece, "The Eskimo is 'pussy.'"

What does this mean? Coward, craven, unmasculine, sissy, queer, gay, pansy, poufter, and so on and so on in that homophobic, illimitless* come down through and polluting the ages.[4]

Now: is the application of this epithet ("pussy") related to the description of our subject as "cold?"

Is there and must there not be a link between the (remarkable) asseveration that the Eskimo is "cold", and that s/he is "pussy"? How could there not be? It would be remiss not to remark it, it would bespeak an ignorance or partiality verging upon† the disqualificatory to ignore it.

And what would it avail?

For the truth, the *truth*, I say, must, and, more importantly, *will* come out.

It's not only "murder" will out, it's murder, incest, rape, and sodomy (consensual or no), fellatio, rimming and browning [. . .][5] and, of course, drunk driving.

Now let is consider the word "is."

Short word, one syllable, sounds like "wiz," "jiz," "quiz," etc.

It is a verb. Which means "a word of doing."

And it is a "world" of doing. It is a busy world.[6]

What can we say to the man or woman who "stays home?"

Not much. Not much, and that grudging and patronizing.

2 – We may safely accept as sufficiently quotidian to lack claim upon our notice the pronouncement that an Eskimo is "cold."[A]
3 – Literary.
4 – Except Ancient Greece. And England.
5 – The following five hundred words were expurgated by the (First) Trilateral Commission, and, though existing on microfiche, were lost in the fire at the Stop 'n' Shop.
6 – Cf. *Encyclopedia Britannica.*

A – See "We Sell Umbrellas When It Rains," in *Jokes of the Catskills* (Animal Welfare League, 1963).

* Limitless. † Surpassing.

Therefore, "Cold Eskimo is pussy."[7]

There was a fellow, hung around the igloo, and was cold. In a land where cold was not remarkable, where *all* were cold.

But he was colder. Why?

He was inactive.

Was he agoraphobic? Lazy? Scared of polar bears,[8] and, therefore, for any of the reasons above, to be scorned?

Scorned, I say, for when has Nature, Eskimo or not, failed to avail itself of any and all societally endorsed opportunities for oppression and evil?*

On the other hand, however, is it not and *always* not *just* this particular creature, this stay-at-home, this supposed laze-about, this coward, shirker, or goldbrick, who brings to us the New Thing, which, in art, commerce, ethics or invention, irreversibly alters our lives?

7 – What can we say about the exclusion from consideration of the sometimes adverb, sometimes adjective, "mighty?" Where might it have fallen in the sentence?[B] For a sometime rambling but, withal, rewarding dispatiation of Greind's "reasoning" for the exclusion, please see *At a Store Near You*, op. cit.
8 – Or seals.

B – Mighty cold Eskimo is pussy.
Cold mighty Eskimo is pussy.
Cold Eskimo mighty is pussy.
Cold Eskimo is mighty pussy.
Cold Eskimo is pussy mighty.

* Never.

A Disquisition on the Uses of Narrative

Though it is not for us to presume, it is unquestionably (or so it seems to this writer) our duty to suggest that the reader may benefit from a brief addendum which, any other than a cursory reading, be assured, will bid fair to [*indecipherable*]

A Disquisition on the Uses of Narrative
or: *Ten Nights in a Turkish Bath*

"What good is it?" or "When is the warder to come?"

So mused the Captain as the day, so long in coming as to have been thought obdurate, crept through the jalousies, throwing that *strié* shadow, now long, now less long, across the floor, where, had those blinds not intruded, he would have perceived – at least in the hours when the sun was low, a semblance of the outline of the Minaret, from which, yes, the muezzin called, when, yes, he, the Captain, woke from what he was surprised to learn had been sleep; for how long and often – at what the absence of his watch could not inform him had been ten, ten-oh-three, ten-oh-five, ten-twelve, etc. – had he wondered, "Will sleep never come?", till he had come to dread it, as a state, of necessity, depriving him of a consciousness which, at the coming of the day, he would most surely and immediately require.

But he had slept. And in his sleep he dreamed.

He dreamed himself back in Hertfordshire, in that corner known as the North Wold, himself a boy, and with his uncle, fishing for the trout, the brown trout, from a bank.

"Well, let us have that ginger beer," his uncle had said, and reached past the boy to the wicker creel.

But then, as if to sturdy himself against some unseen, some unfelt, lurch, his reach shifted, shortened, and his hand came to rest not upon the creel, but, splayed, upon the young boy's crotch.

"Prayer is better than sleep," he could recall the muezzin chanting such a short time ago.

And now the shadow's progress along the floor, and to its junction with the wall, proclaimed the imminence of that time when prayer would be all, and its sequel, an eternity of nothing – the imminence of that which the vizier had referred to as the "interview."

"Shall I be strong?" he thought.

"What are the limits of resistance?" he wondered.

"And to what end? Who would be shamed were it to be a 'womanly performance'? It will be observed by no one save my enemies.

"No record would reach back to any whose opinion I prize, and, finally . . ." he thought, the concept straining the limits of his simple, theretofore unuttered store of philosophy, ". . . finally, I shall be no more."

He dreamed he heard the faint half-note of a bugle.

"No," he thought. "I shall not go that way. Death, yes. But never 'madness.' The regiment is long decamped. There is no possibility that they received my signal. No. *No.* My energies, such as remain, will be not spent in fantasy, but in whatever I may muster of resolve.

"First I must ask forgiveness of whatever powers may be, for my brief (I will grant myself) interregnum of cowardice. It is, of course, first, last, and always, incumbent upon me to 'go game.'"

He thought of a warm Sussex rain, of twenty-two boys in football attire. Tired, hurt, but united in a single desire, to "help the thing along", to "play up, and play the game," and felt again that sharp pain in his side, which had, but not until his appointment in the long vacation, with that Belgian doctor, been revealed to've been a broken rib.

"Hurt, Jimmy?" Blessington had said.

"*Course* it hurts. Isn't it glorious!?"

He could still smell the faint ammoniac odor of the doctor's surgery, the subtle underlying stench of urine, which even the selfless ministrations of the Belgian Sisters could not scour away, and that how-often-thought-of indefinable scent . . . What was it? Lemon? No. It was not lemon. He smiled. For he knew lemon, in its many forms. From the Egypt years. From childhood, in the food, in the air, in the clothing, where the amah had put the dried rinds into the clothes press in the winter months, until the lemon came to be so much a part of him as to be perceived only upon its absence, on his removal to the school.

It was not lemon, he thought, as the doctor's hand, supposed to be engaged in percussion of the chest, descended to his midriff, and beyond, until it grazed the first, soft tendrils of . . .

But wait, but wait – that sound again! Was it a bugle . . .?

No, the wind had shifted. It had blown the sound away. To the north? To the south? Could he frame his mind to compute its direction? And, if so, to what constsructive purpose, save the procrastination of that madness which he felt so fast approaching – the horror of which could but accentuate its approach – his clear awareness of the process of obsession both a component of and the last defense against that shameful delirium he now was sure was to accompany him into the courtyard.

In an hour?

A half-hour?

Could he but strike a bargain with the Almighty, what would he give for the assurance of an hour? Of a mere hour . . . He who had nothing to give, nothing to promise, nothing, oh, nothing in the world save terror and concomitant self-loathing, the last diminishing as the first grew, as if they rested in a balance and himself the fulcrum.

What was that sound?

And why, he asked, and was immediately rewarded with the answer, did he seem to smell beeswax?

The grate shifted in the window, and he saw the form of Nissim, greasing the hinge with a cake of what could only be beeswax, and it transported him back to the vicar's study, the soft, butternut panels of that book-filled room, and the vicar's hand, so lately holding Bishop Atherton's *Ruminations*, descending toward his knee . . . toward . . . *et cetera . . .*

Soap

That which cleanses though,
itself, made from the unclean.
J. COHEN

. . . which is the same problem with the soap, or so it seems to me; for, at what point do we replace it, and in vain to wish one were the sort of folks to melt it down as with those engines seen of old in the downmarket catalogues – to shape it into *what*? *Round* balls? (As if there were any other kind!)

Well-then-I-ask-you. Whilst, on the other hand, the non-disposed has, it has been said, the capacity to indict, as does the other. Indict for the one equally as for the other. For, as and when we let it fester – yes, all innocent, the cleansing agent itself! – it speaks to our capacity for restlessness at the least, and, like it or not, to our social and our economic status.

With the Small, so with the Great. And, sure, there is a point, where, ever the unfortunate, the vestigial, the *blah*-blah, if you will, legacy of one pinko-lefty forebear long passed on and only by that act shut up, where such, I say, such legacy speaks again: "Make it last, make it do, do without", in their one-trick, their weak, their life-long obeisance to their long-past philosophic ancestors, the *workers*. There is a point where even that abusive whine, presented as clear as if harsh philosophy, must, although presented and presenting itself as a friend-of-one's-tribe, must be put upon to stand down and so allow one, in a simple human, unaligned, and, yes, why not, *sui generis*, act, to throw out the soap.

That time must come. Not at the cusp between usefulness and its lack, but no, sufficiently beyond that to have stilled the co-dependent if internal forces of liberal cognition, or, as our time has come to know it, "error."

No. No. There must be some waste. Is not the Perfect (as each civilization frames it) the foe of the Good?

So then if Evil is, as it is, the enemy of Good, and if Perfection is the enemy of Good, what remains to stand as champion of the Good, save the beleaguered, unromantic, pressed and, yes, reviled orphan of metaphysical states, the Good?

So he thought as he looked at the soapdish.

Was it not better to, then, lope along with the gag? As at the Mayan ziggurats, the First World War, the AIDS crisis, the nauseous multitude of invention, and the trillion natural shocks to which we've tried any brief moment, any hour not presently engaged in building up the fire, gathering water, staving off wild beasts?

Was it not then quite the better thing to shrug and throw out the sliver, and change the goddam soap (for, surely, that, of the two, was, of course, less productive of anxiety, or, if you will, productive of less anxiety once the decision had been made), to change the soap, and, for that Sisyphean moment, yes, to commit oneself, not unlike the Hindu Bodhisattva or whatever that Eastern thing may have been called – to the Great Round – the Progression drear enough to make one embrace composting . . .?

Did the soap stand for the human corpse, and was the dialectic, then, between the Christian and the more Judaic view?

So ran his thoughts.

The Old Wrangler

The Old Wrangler

It has become a matter of form to preface any treatment of the subject with the ritual asseveration, "I like the Old Wrangler."

Having acquitted myself, I continue.

I confess that I have a personal connection – not, of course, to the Wrangler himself, but to the phrase.[1]

My father was one of those at the Ski Lift in '98, when the First Fragment was discovered.[2]

1 – Or password.

2 – Note: To have fathered a child who would live till the twenty-second century, a man, by the most liberal estimation, could not have been more than three at the time of the Discovery. And, even granting that to've been the case, would have had to be up sufficiently past his bedtime to have been quite extraordinarily (a) drowsy or (b) cranky.[A]

A – It is, to me, profoundly disturbing that the commentator would not mention the third (and, in all, most likely) possibility, i.e. (c) asleep. I deal with the phenomenon in the next chapter.

How the Old Wrangler and Bootsie Met

These stories are, it has been observed, an inversion–elaboration of the "Bootsie" canon. In *Whence This Sudden Rush of Wings*, in fact, the Old Wrangler (temporarily in the guise of Ting-An-Chou-Tah) himself expatiates (*comme raisonneur*) upon the selfsame subject. I quote (with permission):

"Long ago, when the world was young, before animals could speak, and before *evil* – in the form of Chee-Too-Lan-Wah – entered into hearts of men, there lived a very wise old man."

"What was his name, Grandfather?" little Po Witt said.

"His name," the old man said, "his name was . . ."

Here, of course, occurs the famous "cigarette-burn lacuna," which has permitted a commentator nameless here to advance the theory that the missing name was "Bootsie," this being, should one feel the need for same, a prime, nay, perhaps a perfect, example, to my mind, of "loping the mule."

Why, in a genre piece, where much* care has been taken to construct, if not an accurate, an acceptable, aboriginal tone† – why would the author suggest that a primordial mentor figure bore some public-school cognomen, as if he (the storyteller) referred not to one of the (as it soon is revealed) "gods of the morning" but to his *fag*!!! This beggars imagination.

How can we account for such behavior?

The oh-so-deserved "arrogance, ignorance, self-absorbed fatuity, presumption," etc., can only take one so far; the failure of the psychoanalytic paradigm has, of course, long ceased to be an acceptable subject of parody, let alone scholarship.[1]

1 – Cf. Lon Chaney as *The Wolfman* (Universal, 1940).

* *Too* much. † ???!!!

What remains, save the (religious) platform, view, or intuition of man's inherent worthlessness: *that same issue the Old Wrangler made fair to address!*

What a world.

The Joke Code

The Pet Door

From: *Introduction to the Joke Code* (Sportsman's Press, Undershot, LA, 2131)

The presence of anything is merely the absence of its absence.

Thus to ask, "What can we learn from the absence of *X*?",[1] said question posited as a rhetorical indictment, is to exhibit ignorance of the nature of the world. For things either *are* or *are not* – each state being not merely a complement of the other, but the definition of its *Doppelgänger*.

Binomial theory defines "zero" as being "not one", and the "computer," for all its abominable propensity for evil, defined "lion," charmingly, as "not tiger" ("bear," "plant," "pasta," "color," "idea," "continent," etc.).

Similarly, the genes, the molecules, neutrons, and like minutiae, which are the "building blocks of all life," resolve, and must resolve, in the final analysis into *X* or *0*, "no" or "yes."[2]

You may ask, "What of the indeterminate?"; "What of that which is neither 'yes' nor 'no'?"; "What, finally . . ." – in that which you are free to see as a *reductio ad absurdum* (but is this not a prime tool, not only of the philosophic theorist, but of the matrimonial lawyer?) –

". . . what of 'maybe'?"[3]

1 – *X*, in this case, being the inclusion, in chapter 12, of an other-than-exhaustive litany of the possibilities of portal architecture.
2 – A world-class, screaming tautology, as "the final analysis" is, and may be defined as "that point at which all resolves into *X* or *0*."
3 – The difference between a diplomat and a lady:

When a diplomat says "yes", he means "maybe."
When he says "maybe," he means "no,"
And if he *says* "no," he is no diplomat.
When a lady says "no," she means "maybe."
When she says "maybe," she means "yes."
And if she says "yes," she is no lady.

In which we learn that, at least in two instances, "maybe" exists but as a fiction of the self-delusive.

The world, then, is "yes" or "no," and the *middle* ground is "yes" or "no," as are the questions whether this, this selfsame dictum you read here is "yes" or "no."

And a thing's absence or presence, being indicative one of the other, are the same.[4]

Let us, then, take two seemingly disparate propositions:[5]

1 Never trust a Jew in a bow tie.
2 Women like basketball players, because they dribble before they shoot.

4 – "Things equal to themselves are equal to each other" (Grace Heisenberg, overheard).

5 – The payoff, punchline, or the resolution of his thesis was, of course, lost in the Fire at the Stop 'n' Shop, but has been posited (Jacob Cohen, *Mars and the Asteroids*) thusly:

There *does*, of course, exist a real-life exemplar of "doors within doors." It is the *kitty door.*

Greind, although trapped for eternity in endless space,* most certainly knew of its existence, for it appears on the cover of Item #21260–2, the Comic, *Mr. Natural,* found on the Bookshelf. The omission of the possibility mars his otherwise excellent tome. "Doors within doors" refers, and must refer, to the Kittyport'l®. And, as assuredly, its absence bespeaks a (conscious or no) psychotic antipathy to the feline,[A] or, to put it in

A – See also *Hooray for the Digestive Tract!* (R. Digest Publ., Niceville, N.Y.), from which we quote:

. . . the slap of the waves alongside the dory. "The wind's shifted," he thought. "No, it's definitely backing east."

He raised himself upon his elbow. Slowly, wincing at the pain. He looked down at the blackened flesh, the desiccated, salt-encrusted scab which ringed his wrist – his wrist, which for seventeen years had been chafed by the manacle.

"Better to die out *here*," he thought. "Far better." He was unaware that he'd spoken the thought aloud – so used was he to solitude. But spoken aloud he had, and his speech drew the attention of the sea mew which had – for one day? for three? perched on the gunnel tantalizingly just out of reach.

"Oh, stuff a sock in it," the sea mew drawled. "Whaddaya want, *egg* in your beer? 'F you can't stand the heat, keep out of the kitchen."

"*Go and eat garbage!*" the man screamed. "Pose for eighth-rate holiday painters. I am not at all sure you are not a *dream*."

"Fuck you," the sea mew[A1] said. "Shove it up your ass."

The man lapsed back into what he profoundly hoped was delirium; for he found himself at an amateur production of what even his derangement could not but identify as *The Sound of Music*, by Rodgers and Hammerstein.

A1 – For a further treatment of the sea mew, see J. J. Audubon, *Birds of the Atlantic Corridor*.

* Aren't we all?

---

its best possible light, a prejudice against cats.[B]

A very fat lady carrying a Brownie[A2] squeezed in front of him. "I didn't know," he thought, "the World held that much Calico . . ."[A3]

B – What does the above say of the author's "felinist" omission of the possibility that the pet door might accommodate a *ferret*? *

A2 – See 'The Best Christmas Present of Them All'.
A3 – The Calico appears again, of course, in *Rybecki's Dream: Night Two – The Mud on the Spikes Explained.*[A3A]

A3A – It does, indeed, but as the name of Rybecki's *cat*. Has this writer no self-*respect*? That is the answer I am left with. Either that or brigands burst into his house and chained him to the toilet, or threatened to kill his maid unless he penned a stupid and spurious note. Is our life not complex enough, without this wilful "muddying of the Waters"?[A3A1]

A3A1 – The editor responds: "Yes, 'Calico' was the name of Rybecki's cat. And *Waters* was the name of his *butler*. But do *I* jump all over *you*, you stupid *shithead*? (From "This Correspondence Now Must Cease", *Bongazine* All-Rybecki issue, fall '09.

* Or, more to the point, a dog.

From Muuguu

"Thoughts on Awakening"

There is no Joke Code.
There is no Inner Code.
There is no Capsule.
There is no Mall.
Now there is naught but grim
Denial. Now there is not even that.[1]

WALTER STEVENS, *MUUGUU*

1 – Oft quoted as the "False Anagram Pastiche," for the last two "ND" lines, its celebrity is, of course, "a shuck," as "Denial," rightly, belongs as the last word in the *second* to last line; and, *plus* which, even if not, *so what*, as what could it mean that there was a poem the last two lines of which began with the letters "ND"? So what? *Anyone* could write one. Look here:

Get out of bed.
Go to the head.
Now blow your brains out.
Dead, dead, dead.

You get my point?

The Missing Page

The Missing Page
Greind

He wrote that he hoped there "would be found that fragment which would make the whole thing whole."[1] How close his dream came to fruition!

And how differently it might have ended had the Woman in the Bookstore not forgotten her bag.

What is Chance? What is Coincidence?

How often do we curse the apparently accidental, only to find, in retrospect, that we beheld, in fact, the operations of our own character, or the will of some superior Force or Being – or, if you will, the great, the ultimate confluence of the two, which confluence reveals us – not less than the object of our wonder or investigation – to be part of the Whole.

It has been suggested,[2] of course, that Bennigsen was *himself* the "missing page"; that it was only in his "self" that the disparate elements were "made whole."

The sounds themselves are not displeasing, certainly, but what do these words *mean*?

And, *should* they be found, by the jejune, sententious, academic, bored or criminal mind, to possess meaning, does his death not beg the question?

The Page is Game
The Age is Gone
The Wisdom of the Sage is Gone.[3]

1 – *Tales of the Old Wrangler.*
2 – "Ode to the Missing Page," in D. Wheeler (ed.), *The World's Worst Poems* (Bobbs, Merril, 2021).
3 – Ibid.

And Bennigsen (Greind) is gone.

"And we are left to weep,"[4] laments the herald, and we find in the next column, TWELVE-YEAR-OLD BOY BUILDS WIND-POWERED SCOOTER.

But, looking back, he must have seen that, looking back, it had been inexplicable, for what could explain it?

Save the human capacity to find safety in amalgamation, trusting, as any animal, to the multiplied force of the individual survival mechanism.

But the survival mechanism in their case was just intelligence – which, in groups much larger than a dinner party, can only become consensus.

The individual responds earlier to danger than the group.

The individual who responds earliest (i.e., most effectively to danger) would be that possessed of the best, the most acute senses – the highest capacity for flight, ferocity, etc. Among the human beings, however, the individual lauded as most prescient is not him of the greatest intelligence, but him with the most power to convince.

So, it was that combination which led to the species' demise.

Their intelligence enabled them (potentially) to assess and withstand a threat. But the survival of the herd instinct led them to squander any advantage in obedience to (what they each hoped was) the will of the group.

And humans, being what they are, learn they can achieve status and power through the manipulation of the falsification/fabrication of consensus.

Such were not only incapable of but uninterested in threat assessment (i.e., the health of the species) but only in their individual survival and prominence.

And their survival skill was, again, not that of the group to which they belonged (intelligence), but that of the rogue: distraction, falsification and treachery. And their power came, strangely, from a lack of fellow feeling, enabling them to exploit.

4 – Subhead obituary, "The Death of Bennigsen," *New York Times.*

They had nothing to offer save the false assurance that they spoke for the group. They were good, in short, only at "getting elected."

Now, the horror felt at that time by the general (cf. the Cola Riots) has been (rightly) said to've been a displacement over the wellnigh two hundred years of what they were pleased to call "advertising." Whomever it was – he or she can only be accounted a visionary – who discerned that the process of statistical analysis *itself* engendered such a feeling of awe in the public, that, rather than cast oneself on the mercy of statistical "results," one could with, indeed, *less* expenditure of effort, simply elect which course he wished the populace to pursue, and publish "facts" designed "to make the sheep obey" – that person who saw the superfluity of the intermedian step – that person was a genius.

. . . in the place where it all meets. Where this would become clear: that we were enjoined to be patient not until things should improve, but until they should be over.

Then what difference in a length of life? For, in eternity consciousness must leach away – for how could we be conscious through eternity?[5]

That being so, what was the "intermediary term"? What was the length of life sufficient to the mortal mind? Something "longer than *this*," but not indefinitely expansible?

What was that length? Or, if one could deduce that it did not exist, then was not all anxiety revealed as greed? Greed for sensation? Could one not, then, theoretically, banish it by an act of will? Could one not perceive that the "necessary term"[6] was not a "length of days," but a state of peace? And could one not, again, and always, theoretically, replace "greed for sensation" with "longing for peace?"

Or, absent the strength to proclaim it, that that magic term, the Missing Page, at which one would announce, "I've had enough," was a

5 – Not a convincing argument – we could be; it might be boring, but we could be . . .

6 – The "necessary term" was, of course, a password of the early Clubs. It was identified, by them, with the "Missing Page," and there is some evidence that it described a super- or infra-cabal of initiates dedicated to a reconstruction of the Joke Code. This is generally accepted as its earliest verifiable use.

function not of time, but of will . . . would that perception render it incumbent upon one either to embrace or to renounce that same apotheosis?

Greed, Greed. Greed mingled with fear. Like the bored, disaffected rich – who long for the new thing but lack the courage to renounce the old – who lounge in terrible, in maddening, in soul-destroying luxury, repining for that release which they must know will come, if it comes, not from novelty (for what is novelty to them but repetition?) but from renouncement, from . . .

"Ben? Ben? Shut up," Roger said.[7]

7 – Walt Whitman, "O Cocksuckers", *Bongazine*, no. 232, "All Whitman" issue: "Lost, Lost for All Time . . ."

QUESTION: If lost for once, might we not say, "lost for all time"?
ANSWER: No. As in the case of if you lost your car keys and you didn't know where they were* and, then, later on, you found them.

Scottie Grootch, Eugene, OR.[A]

A – It is notable that the Redactor took this prime example of "Rogue Responsa" to heart sufficiently to respond. We here reprint his "Letter to Scottie":

Dear Scottie,

Thank you for your interest in my work. I am touched and pleased that you took the time to write.

Forgive me if I infer from your handwriting and syntax that you are not "fully grown to Man's Estate."

Do you have a dog?[A1] What kind?

What sort of things do you like to do "for fun"?

Write and tell a lonely old man, would you?

Greind

A1 – "If so" missing? Deleted?[A1A]

A1A – Missing, yes. But how remarkable that its absence is merely noted *in passing*. For does it† not bespeak a longing, no, a *hunger* for the Canine? How touching, how dear. How *humanizing* – "Do you have a dog? What kind?"

* Redundant. † Its absence.

L'Envoi

L'Envoi: The Noted Fighting Prowess of the Cottage Queen

Cut into the Plinth, on the Mall. This quotation, awarded the highest endorsement of its universality, is there found, unattributed. Any schoolchild, in the Time Before the Riots, would have looked at a request for its source as the act of a madman.[1] And it was, in fact, this request which alerted, first, Billy, and, then, the Park Police to the arrival, in their midst, of the Old Wrangler.[2]

When cornered, like the boar, the stoat, the bull, the cottage queen, it has been noted throughout history, will turn and fight.

Sun Tsu, in his *Art of War*, cautions to leave one's adversary a "golden bridge" over which he may retreat. Its absence, he avers, must at the last prolong and may, in fact, unbalance any conflict, tipping the scales of victory away from the stronger, and toward the more ferocious. So with the cottage queen, discovered at his moment of pleasure,[3] nay, perhaps at the zenith, or the apogee of the aforesaid moment, as the Vice Squad, in their butch black jackets, kicks in the door (would it have killed them to have knocked?) (or were they brought up in a *barn*???), now roused to fury, and his very lust, if you will, but seeking a new channel, for, crested, as it was, unable to subside, turned from

1 – The quotation is found in the second book of Jane of Trent, in chapter 5, "Chet Seeks Comfort." For a fuller understanding of the quotation, and its, to our mind, unaccountable – affection is hardly a strong enough word to the pre-Riot mind – I will make bold to remind the reader of one slim volume found on the Shelf in the Capsule: *Beef Encounter*, with its stained and dog-eared pages, bespeaking not only its place in the heart of Greind, but his enduring love of literature.

2 – "Well, hello," the old man said, "and who might *you* be?"

"I, I'm *Billy*," I responded. But as I looked at his eyes, my certainty fled. Who *was* this "Billy"; what was "I," and what was this once essential, now obviously absurd, separation between sentient beings? Were we not all Part of the One? And was this knowledge not my joy, as I sloughed what I had, mistakenly, understood as my personality, and knew, at once, the Greater Thing?

"Do you like country music?" he said.

"I don't know, sir," I said. "It very much depends on the artist." And then the moment was gone.

3 – Cf. *A Ream is a Wish Your Heart Makes*, op. cit.

its proper debouchment, bay, tidewater, egress, in short, but yet still mounting, must, like that same aqueous element invoked in this conceit, discover or fashion a new escapement. Roused, I say, to a perhaps previously unsuspected pitch of bellicosity, the spirit turns from the quest for flesh to the pursuit of blood.

Where the Sea Ends, There the Land Begins*

"Or, perhaps, it all comes to naught."

"No, no, there's no 'perhaps' about it," Chet said. "No 'perhaps' about it, Ging— . . . *Look out the window.*"

Ginger did as she was asked, and there she saw the surf on the shingle, pounding the rocks into sand, drawing the sand back to redistribute it.

"To what end?" she wondered. "To what end . . .?"

She felt assured that Chet would draw his text from it, and illuminate it in some way she'd, perhaps, "seen," but never before "noted."

What, she wondered, would he adopt for his subject? The interconnectedness of the organic and the inorganic, perhaps.

She mused on the obviously constant flux of a life, of a world, of an existence each attempted – some through philosophy, some through neurosis, some by science or art, to capture – through that skill and for that moment sufficient to bring them a compass of peace, to still the nagging anomie for that one millisecond, and denominate it triumph. Or would he adopt the ever fruitful "evolution" as his theme – the restless, constant change, elaboration, decay, renaissance, in all that lived?

Or, could it be, she wondered, that his subject would be the interface, that less-than-real, that, finally, imaginary intersect between the sea and land; or the mimetic "breath" of the sea, as it expanded and contracted once again into itself?

"It is going to piss down out there," Chet exclaimed, and farted.

Who were these demi-gods? These – the late twenty-first century mind-habitants of the Pantheon – Donna, and Chet, and the ever-allusive Ginger – who *were* these, whose, finally, domestic squabbles, offered, to that time, a "new vision" of the world?

For, is the human mind not constantly reiterating the familial constellation?[1]

1 – Carl Rogers, *Go to Your Room*, op. cit.

* Generally accounted "the world's most useless motto."

Now, as the Ancient Geeks, now as the "Tribes," of Jewry, now as the signs of the Zodiac, now as the "residents," or the Books in the Capsule.

Did Ginger actually exist?

There are, of course, two answers. They are "yes," and "no," and these two answers are traditional.

There is a third: "What difference?"

She "exists" now. She "holds the place," or, more to the point, her Canon holds, or awards to her (and, by extension, of course, to her Adherents) the place of the Trickster: of Loki, Raven, Pan, who "created the worlds," or Brer Fox, Léon Blum, *et cetera.*

It is her "job" to confound, confront, and, through these operations, to *create* that primordial state, that chaos from which, and only from which "the new thing" can arise.*

The Trickster, stealing corn from the farmers, fire from the gods, pages from the Manuscript, this, then, is Ginger, for whom "mischief" always comes first. This is her office in the Canon. It is this for which we are indebted to her, as she embodies for her time, and, so for us, who have enshrined it, the virtues of non-virtue, the wisdom of folly, the instructive component of misadventure, the teleological worth of chaos. This is Ginger.

We contend, here below, each in himself, and, in the macro-consciousness, between the poles "Yes, I shall do it!" and "Oh, what the hell."

"It is this dialectic moves the whole thing on."[2]

Here we have Eros and Thanatos, Reason and Wit, in flux, before us, much as the sea over which Ginger mused, awaiting "Chet's final verdict" on "the cause of it all"; and, as in the myth, it is her disappointment which gives rise (in the Canon) to the Adventure of the Boathouse, and in the larger picture, to the world at large.

For her "Flight up the Hill" is none other than Raven's rocketing egress from the Underworld, Prometheus' (questionable) gift of fire from on high, the opening of Pandora's box, or Greind's "Discovery of the Season Tickets" – it is the necessary interjection of that final, last, unnamed and sacrosanct, prerogative of the Ineffable.

2 – T. E. Lawrence, *Seven Pails Full of Wisdom.*

* But who, then, for the love of Christ, is "Chet"?

The End of the Day

Selah

Or, at the end of the day, we might identify Jane of Trent with (as) the Lady of Spain. We might identify her, with more hope of popular acceptance, but, finally, with not one whit more justification* with Lola Montez, or with the Mother of God. Why not? When all is, finally, arbitrary; for the *frisson* between the given word and individual discovery or intuition is, itself, open both to interpretation of dismissal, based, yet again, on some adoption or admixture of those selfsame forces which it presents itself to treat.

For how do we feel the processes of cognition? By retreat (yoga, tai-chi, ga-wong-ta, psychotomimetic pharmaceuticals, etc.) by flight, study or absorption in those states wherein that same oblivion, that same selflessness, Nirvana, sense of non-being, becomes, at its fullest, nothing but a (granted, perhaps or necessarily, inchoate) intuition, understanding, revelation or, to make an end, knowledge. What a thing! And how we yearn (do we not, I think we do) to discover and appeal to that higher self, tradition, or being, which would both strive and instruct[1] us.

Did the Toll Hound dance? Why? What can it matter? At the end of the day? That such and such a one knew this or that: the history of the Western Plains, the uses of bowline-on-a-bight, the secret vice of "Bootsie,"[2] the (lost) ground plan of the Stop 'n' Shop, etc., till the mind – for *past* rebellion – turns upon itself, not in disgust, but triumph, and that day is done.

1 – And absolve.

2 – How secret could it have been, with the servants all around the whole time? See *T'aint Easy Being Rich* by "A Gentleman's Gentleman" (Viscount Hault, 15th Earl of Kent).

* Too true.

The Poem Reiterated

The Poem Reiterated

D awn, and the nascent, roseate glow.
F riend, if thou art Friend, perchance Foe,
S tand with me in the Light which sootheth all,
S uffusing the now ended slumbers on The Mall.

Only conceive, if it is granted thee,
Those noted years of bootless Misery,
The trials of the Heads of State,
The ceaseless Perturbation of the Great,

The ponderous burden of the few
To license, nay, inaugurate the new
Peregrinations of the Wandering Jew.

But for a moment meditate, I pray,
But for a moment stay.
Encapsulate the figures carved in stone,
Picture the absent flesh, the buried bone,
Hear with your inner hearing that fell tone
Of those controlled by Lust alone,
Of those whom neither shame nor pride debars
From luxury in the vermilion sway of Mars.
Apostrophize, if you will, on the thrall
Of History, and upon the futility of all.

T hen may my eyes meet yours. And, for that while,
O , brother, may we not essay a smile?
L ost in the maelstrom of time,
L inked for a heartbeat sublime

H eld for the sake of what O'erarching All –
O f what imponderables burnt –
U pon the deepest revelation of them all . . .

Closing Note

Closing Note

It was not, of course, Jane of Trent. The rhyme could not have been Jane of Trent, as her cult, long discredited, had become, in the era of the Poem's composition, anathema.

Brave would have been the soul, indeed, who'd dare to allude, with however many layers of deniability, to her, or her (then, of course, moot) "Place on the Mall."

That the Poem was a cunning fabrication was doubted by no one at the time of its "discovery." It passed from view, in the words of one contemporary historian, because "it just wasn't funny";[1] and the work here reproduced[2] is offered by the editors as a *bonne bouche*, a loving look at a curious Time Past.

The Editors offer and endorse it not as a work of scholarship[3] but, perhaps, as a fit object of study. If not of study, then of contemplation. If not of contemplation, then of wistful sadness, at the oversight, loss, or dismission, or, to put a good face on it, subsumption in the general whole which must be the eventual lot of all.[4]

1 – "Hold on to yer seats!", *Bongazine*, Halloween issue, October 2012.

2 – *Wilson.*

3 – The Redactor was, of course, [*indecipherable*].

4 – Omitted from this edition are the Editor's Acknowledgments, and the "notorious" reference to "Bootsie in the Royal Navy," which can be found as a footnote to the errata insert in the unbound galleys of the author's *Yo Ho Ho: Banned, Burnt and Discredited: Smut of the Sea* (Progress Publishing House, Neopalatinsk): "Is anybody *there* . . . is anybody *there* . . . is anybody *there* . . .?"[A]

A – The rest of the transmission was, of course, but the persistence of the carrier tone, the "three bursts of sound," and, then, what that age had come to call "The Silence."

The End

Three
From "Weebut's Selected 'Thoughts from the Diary'"

"Febr. Elevn [*sic*] = 2.11.2033 = 2+1+1+2+0+3+3 = 12 = 1+2 = 3. But what does '3' equal?" she said. And so we have the beginning of Modern Numerology. Or, as she wrote, "On this spot was revealed to Ginger H. Kahn the meaning of numbers."

We have seen it graven on the Monument, we've seen it* printed on mugs, caps, clothing and banners, sold (under license) on the Mall; we've seen it parodied and lampooned (to cite one vulgar example) upon underwear, where "this spot" is clearly made to refer to the nipples or to genitalia. It has been part of the white or "background" noise of civilization – a catch phrase of the class of "What a shockingly bad hat!", or "*And* they are mild" – those tags of yore, now famous, like the Gabor Sisters,[1] for being famous.

11 February 2033. A simple date. In which she professed to've found mystical meaning – upon which meaning an entire branch of science was established, which meaning, which discipline, which knowledge we now see subsiding, once again, into nothingness.

And nothing will remain.

Neither her insights nor her self-doubt. Neither the clarifications nor the misreadings of her biographers. Finally, not the number 3, nor the propensity nor the capacity of the human mind to perceive or impose order upon that universe which may exist, if it exists at all, but as a freak of an electric system out of control – sprung into being to aid in the production or capture of food, and warped (by what process we cannot say) into a self-elaborating instrument of destruction, hastening, finally, the dissolution both of itself and its host.[2]

1 – Meaning uncertain. Poss. astrol.?
2 – The (disputed) passage continues:

---

* The phrase.

—
Oh, but, oh, we're happy . . .! Why complain? Then let us sit down a while. I don't regret coming at all. (*He rummages in his sack.*) Would you like an apple . . .?